Too many of us, regardless of our familiarity with the stories of the Bible, are blind to the story of the Bible. We miss the forest for the trees. We fail to recognize how the Bible's many individual stories fit together to tell one mega-story. The macro-story. The story of God and us.

Phil Vischer
Creator of Veggie Tales and What's in the Bible? video series

Jim Nicodem's purpose is to lay out, in straightforward, nontechnical language, many of the most important principles of interpretation. He does this so each person may know the foundational principles of biblical interpretation, and so understand many texts. In other words, Jim wants the church he serves, and many other churches, to be filled with men and women who will become better Bible readers.

D. A. Carson, PhD
Research Professor of New Testament at Trinity Evangelical Divinity School, Author of New Testament Commentary Survey

As a university professor on a Christian college campus, I can tell you that biblical illiteracy is on the rise. That's why the Bible Savvy series should be a prerequisite reading for everyone. Jim Nicodem puts the cookies on the bottom shelf by making the epic story of the biblical narrative understandable and accessible. The Bible Savvy series lays out the foundation and context for God's Word and then shows us in plain language how to apply the Bible's teachings to our lives step-by-step. It's phenomenal.

Les Parrott, PhD
Seattle Pacific University
Author of You're Stronger Than You Think

The Bible is one of the most precious possessions to a believer living in a restricted nation. I am constantly amazed by the hunger for biblical teaching expressed by those who face persecution daily. Their sacrificial passion should inspire us to rekindle our quest for biblical understanding. Jim Nicodem's Bible Savvy series is the kind of resource needed to reengage our hearts and minds with God's Word, and renew a hunger for God's truth on par with our persecuted brother and sisters.

James E. Dau
President, The Voice of the Martyrs

Jim has done a masterful job in the Bible Savvy series! In these four concise books, Jim marches with clarity and skill into topics that would be difficult to tackle in a seminary classroom, much less in an American living room. And rather than a monologue, these books create a dialog among the author, the reader, their small group, and the living Word of God. These practical, approachable resources provide foundational training that is greatly needed by nearly every small group and leader I encounter.

Greg Bowman
Coauthor of *Coaching Life-Changing Small Group Leaders*
Past executive director of the Willow Creek Association

Reading the four books in the Bible Savvy series is like getting a Bible college education in a box! The Lord is calling our nation to a Bible reading revolution, and these books are an invitation to be part of it.

Hal Seed
Author of *The Bible Questions* and *The God Questions*
Lead Pastor, New Song Community Church, Oceanside, California

Living in the land of the Bible is considered a privilege by many, but the real privilege is to let the Bible become alive through us, in whatever land we may live. In the Bible Savvy series, Jim Nicodem not only helps us to understand God's plan to save us, but also His desire to change and shape us through His Word and Spirit in order to be a light in this dark world.

Rev. Azar Ajaj
Vice President and lecturer, Nazareth Evangelical Theological Seminary

To ignite a love for the God's Word in others is the goal of any spiritual leader. Communicating God's Word is the most important of all. Pastor Jim's Bible Savvy series is the tool, the guide, and the process for worship leaders to go into deep spiritual places. His biblical scholarship, communicated with such creativity, is exactly what is needed in worship ministry today.

Stan Endicott
Slingshot group coach/mentor
Worship Leader, Mariners Church, Irvine, California

Jim Nicodem leads one of America's finest churches. Jim knows how to communicate the truth of the Bible that brings historical knowledge with incredible practical application. The Bible Savvy series is the best I have ever seen. Your life and faith will be enhanced as you use and apply this material to your life.

> Jim Burns, PhD
> President, HomeWord
> Author of *Creating an Intimate Marriage* and *Confident Parenting*

Pastor Nicodem is like a championship caliber coach: he loves to teach, and he stresses that success comes from mastering the basics. The Bible Savvy series will help you correctly interpret the best Playbook ever written: the Bible. Understanding and applying its fundamentals (with the help of the Bible Savvy series) will lead one to the Ultimate Victory . . . eternity with Jesus.

> James Brown
> Host of *The NFL Today* on the CBS television network

Walk

How to Apply the Bible

James L. Nicodem

MOODY PUBLISHERS
CHICAGO

© 2013 by
James L. Nicodem

All Scripture quotations are taken from the *Holy Bible, New International Version*®, NIV®. Copyright © 1973, 1978, 1984 by Biblica, Inc.™ Used by permission of Zondervan. All rights reserved worldwide.

Published in association with the literary agency of Wolgemuth & Associates, Inc.

Edited by Jim Vincent
Interior design: Ragont Design
Cover design: Smartt Guys design
Cover image: iStockphoto

Library of Congress Cataloging-in-Publication Data

Nicodem, James L., 1956-
    Walk : how to apply the Bible / James L. Nicodem.
        pages cm. — (The Bible savvy series)
    Includes bibliographical references.
    ISBN 978-0-8024-0636-1
    1. Bible—Hermeneutics. 2. Bible—Criticism, interpretation, etc.
    I. Title.
    BS476.N53 2013
    220.6—dc23
                                                            2012047219

We hope you enjoy this book from Moody Publishers. Our goal is to provide high-quality, thought-provoking books and products that connect truth to your real needs and challenges. For more information on other books and products written and produced from a biblical perspective, go to www.moodypublishers.com or write to:

Moody Publishers
820 N. LaSalle Boulevard
Chicago, IL 60610

1 3 5 7 9 10 8 6 4 2

Printed in the United States of America

About the
Bible Savvy Series

I MET THE REAL ESTATE AGENT at my front
door and invited him in. My wife and I were about to put
our home on the market and I had called Jeff as a potential
representative. As he sat down at our dining room table and
opened his briefcase, I noticed a Bible perched on top of other
papers. I asked Jeff if he was a Bible reader and he replied that
he was just getting started. What had prompted his interest?
He'd recently come across a list in *Success, Inc.* magazine of
the most influential books recommended by business leaders.
The Bible had been the most frequently mentioned book on
the list. So, Jeff was going to give it a try.

My real estate agent isn't alone in his new interest in the
Bible. According to a recent survey, 91 percent of those who
have lately begun attending church were motivated to do so
by a desire to understand what the Bible has to say to their
lives.[1] That means nine of every ten visitors to church are in-
trigued by the Bible! But while they are curious about God's
Word, they're also a bit intimidated by it. The Bible is such
a daunting book, written in ancient times and addressed to

vastly different cultures. Is it really possible to draw relevant insights from it for our lives today? People are returning to church to find out.

Ironically, while an interest in Bible knowledge can be detected among those who are new to church, it seems to be on the wane among many veteran churchgoers. When my oldest daughter enrolled at a Christian college, the president of the school addressed parents on opening day. He told us that the Bible comprehension exams of each incoming class of freshmen show less and less knowledge of God's Word. And then he added: "These kids are growing up in *your* churches." Evidently, many churches are not doing a good job of teaching committed believers how to read, interpret, and apply the Bible.

The Bible Savvy series has been written to help a wide spectrum of Bible readers—from newbies to seasoned Bible study leaders—get their arms around God's Word. This multi-book series covers four essential Bible-related topics that Moody Publishers has made available in one set as a comprehensive manual for understanding God's Word and putting it into practice. *Walk* is the final book of the four-book series.

An added bonus to the Bible Savvy series is the Study Guide that follows every chapter of each book. These questions for personal reflection and group discussion have been crafted by a team of small-groups experts. The Study Guide is also available online at biblesavvy.com and may be downloaded and used for personal study or reproduced for members of a small group.

Four Things You Must Know to
Get the Most out of God's Word

The four books of the Bible Savvy series will give you a grasp of the following topics, allowing God's Word to become a rich resource in your life:

1. *The storyline of the Bible.* The Bible is actually a compilation of sixty-six books that were written over a 1,500-year period. But amazingly there is one central storyline that holds everything together. You'll trace this storyline in *Epic* from Genesis to Revelation, learning how each of the sixty-six books contributes to the overall plot.

2. *The reliability of the Bible.* How did God communicate what He wanted to say through human authors? What are the evidences that the Bible is a supernatural book? How do we know that the *right* books made it into the Bible and that the *wrong* books were kept out of it? Isn't a text that was hand-copied for hundreds of years bound to be filled with errors? *Foundation* will give you answers to questions like

these—because you won't get much out of the Bible until you're certain that you can trust it.

3. *How to understand the Bible*. People read all sorts of crazy things into the Bible, and have used it to support a wide variety of strange (and sometimes reprehensible) positions and activities. In *Context* you will learn the basic ground rules for accurately interpreting Scripture. (Yes, there are rules.)

4. *How to apply the Bible*. It's one thing to read the Bible, and it's another thing entirely to walk away from your reading with an application for your life. Even members of Bible study groups occasionally do a poor job of this. Participants leave these gatherings without a clear sense of how they're going to put God's Word into practice. *Walk* will equip you to become a Bible doer.

Do You Have Savvy?

The dictionary defines *savvy* as *practical know-how*. It is my hope and prayer that the Bible Savvy series will lead you into an experiential knowledge of God's Word that will transform your life.

Many people have contributed to my own love and understanding of the Bible over the years—as well as to the writing of this book. I owe a huge debt of gratitude to them.

Mom and Dad made God's Word central to our family life, encouraging my siblings and me to memorize big chunks of it.

When I got to high school, I was a bit turned off to church, but I started attending a youth ministry in a neighboring suburb that was led by Bill Hybels. (These were pre–Willow Creek Community Church days, when dinosaurs roamed the earth.) Bill had (and still has) an incredible ability to open the Bible, read a passage out loud, and then drive home its application to the lives of his listeners. After a year of hearing him teach God's Word in such a life-impacting way, I went away to college and decided to major in biblical studies.

Two professors (among many) fanned the flame of my love for the Bible during my college and seminary years. Dr. Gerry Hawthorne taught me Greek New Testament at Wheaton College, and there are thousands of men and women in ministry around the world today who still remember his simple-but-powerful class devotions. He'd put one verse on the chalkboard (remember chalk?) and then tease out its significance for our lives—often with tears in his eyes. Dr. D. A. Carson taught me the Bible at Trinity Evangelical Divinity School. His books (and occasional phone and email exchanges) continue to shape me today. I aspire to have even a quarter of his passion for God's Word!

After school, as I started out in youth ministry, I began listening to cassette tapes (same era as chalk) by Dr. John

MacArthur. John is internationally famous for his verse-by-verse teaching of Scripture. Although he is occasionally more adamant about certain doctrines than I am (we agree on the essentials), his love for the Bible is infectious. John has set the bar high for all pastors who want to faithfully teach their churches God's Word. As my ministry has continued, I have found other communicators who whet my appetite for Scripture—many of them through their books, some of them currently through their podcasts. Thank you Lee Strobel, Joe Stowell, John Ortberg, Mark Driscoll, Francis Chan, Tim Keller, and many others.

Today, my desire to get people into the Bible is fueled by the five thousand-plus eager learners whom I have the privilege of pastoring at Christ Community Church of St. Charles, Illinois, and its regional campuses. I am especially grateful for both the staff and volunteer leaders who oversee almost four hundred Community Groups that are studying God's Word. And one of those leaders, who writes incredible Bible curricula and teaches scores of Bible-hungry women, is my wife, Sue. Her devotion to Scripture is a constant inspiration to me.

Lastly, a special thanks to my faithful assistant, Angee Jenkins, who helped to edit my manuscript, track down footnotes, and protect my writing time; and to my agent, Andrew Wolgemuth, who found a great publisher in Moody to make the Bible Savvy series available to you.

*To watch Jim's personal introduction to Walk,
scan the QR code below with your smartphone or go to
www.biblesavvy.com/video/#walk1.*

Contents

Foreword

JIM NICODEM HAS done a great job in the Bible Savvy series of demonstrating that the Bible is a special book whose storyline is compelling, whose content is reliably authoritative, and whose history and theology is understandable. But as good as the first three books have been, it would be of no avail if Jim hadn't made it all the way to this closing volume in the series. Digesting the earlier books equips us to move confidently into Scripture to harvest fascinating truths about God and ourselves. But if all we have at the end is a bucket load of knowledge, we have missed the point!

God never intended that the Bible would simply make us smart—although that is a part of the process. If all we have is knowledge of what is true and right from God's point of view, then we are in a dangerous place. Knowledge left to itself will make us proud of what we know and judgmental toward those who are biblically ignorant. Instead, God gave us the His Word to transform our lives—to move us from assimilation to application so that in the end we can reflect His glory by becoming conformed to the image of Jesus Christ.

But applying the transforming truth of Scripture is a challenge. A challenge because the process begins with the convicting power of God's Word which, like a mirror, shows us what we really are like and what needs to be changed. When you got up this morning and looked in the mirror you immediately knew that you needed to do something about it . . . and everyone around you was glad that you did.

Do your world and the testimony of Christ through you a favor and surrender to the life changing influence of the Bible. In our fallen state we are not prone to forgiveness, grace, mercy, patience, generosity, unconditional love and a host of other virtues that make your life a blessing to others and a credit to God. Applying divine truth to our anything-but-divine lives will in the end make us humble about ourselves and compassionate toward others.

With the assistance of the indwelling Spirit, an open Bible on your lap and Pastor Nicodem's handy volume nearby, open your heart and let the transforming work of God's Word do its work!

JOSEPH STOWELL
President, Cornerstone University

Introduction:
"So What?"

I WENT STRAIGHT FROM being a biblical studies major in college (where I wrestled with Scripture in the original Hebrew and Greek) to being a youth pastor in a church (where I taught the Bible to middle school and high school students). What an abrupt transition!

Those kids weren't particularly interested in how the tense of a Greek verb impacted something Paul wrote in one of his epistles. They were preoccupied with gaining popularity at school, making it onto the basketball team, following their favorite band, and finishing their homework before the weekend was over. How could I teach them God's Word in a way that would be relevant to their everyday lives?

Being newly married at the time, I took advantage of my wife's wise input as I prepared my weekly talks for these students. I remember sitting Sue down on the threadbare sofa in our sparsely furnished apartment and making her listen to parts of each message before I went public with them. Then I would ask her for feedback.

Almost always, the first thing out of her mouth was a two-word question: "So what?"

"What do you mean, 'so what'?" I would shoot back, feeling defensive.

She would then patiently explain that my talk hadn't clearly called for an application. What was my text from the Bible challenging these students to do? What was the *so what* of my presentation?

While I was frequently annoyed with Sue for pointing out this recurring deficiency in the rough drafts of my talks, I knew she was putting her finger on something very important. James warns us in his New Testament epistle, "Do not merely listen to the word, and so deceive yourselves. Do what it says" (James 1:22). The end result of exposure to the Bible—whether by listening, reading, or studying—should be the application of what it teaches. What will we put into practice? How will we *walk* the Word?

Walk is the final book in the Bible Savvy series. It is the culmination of everything that has been taught in the first three books about grasping the Bible's storyline (*Epic*), trusting the reliability of the Bible's text (*Foundation*), and interpreting each Bible passage according to sound hermeneutics (*Context*). Yet none of this has lasting impact on our lives if we don't walk away from each encounter with God's Word prepared to do something in response to it. Unfortunately, what the text is asking you to do will not always be readily apparent. Coming up with applications that fit your life's circumstances is a learned skill. *Walk* will give you the steps for acquiring that skill.

Light for the Path

IF YOU EVER GET THE opportunity to visit Israel, make sure you visit Hezekiah's Tunnel—but bring a flashlight with you! Otherwise you will walk in complete darkness during your tunnel tour. The tunnel, located on the south side of the old city of Jerusalem, was constructed back in 700 BC by Israel's King Hezekiah as he was getting ready for an Assyrian invasion.

Jerusalem's major water supply at the time was the Gihon Spring, which, unfortunately, was located *outside* the city walls. That's not a good spot for your major water supply if your city is about to come under siege!

So King Hezekiah covered over the Gihon Spring and began building an underground aqueduct to divert the water to a pool (the Pool of Siloam) *inside* the city walls. One team of underground diggers started at the spring, while the other team started at the pool—and they somehow managed to meet in the middle! The finished aqueduct, five hundred yards long, was an engineering marvel in 700 BC.

Besides bringing a flashlight for your tunnel tour, be ready to walk through knee-deep, icy cold water for forty-five minutes. I emphasize that flashlight because I remember Sue and I didn't have one when we made our trek through the tunnel a couple of summers ago. We were enrolled in a course at Jerusalem University College with forty other students, so we were counting on others in the class to come prepared. Only a few of them were. (Where are the Boy Scouts when you need them?)

It was a really, really dark and claustrophobic walk for most of the way. Our only consolation was knowing that if we kept moving forward—and the walls were so narrow and the ceiling was so low at times that forward was the only direction we *could* move—we would eventually end up at our destination. Yup, next time we'll bring a flashlight!

Turn On the Light!

Hezekiah's Tunnel is a metaphorical picture of our lives. On any given day, we can feel like we're in desperate need of light. There's a big decision looming in front of us, or we're in the middle of a crisis, or we're struggling in our parenting, or we're trying to figure out a career path, or there's conflict and confusion in some important relationship. And we're just not sure what to do next. We're *in the dark*, as the saying goes. We wish somebody would shine a little light on our path.

Well, that's exactly what God offers to do. The light that He shines is the light of His Word. In Psalm 119:105, the psalmist says to God: "Your word is a lamp to my feet and a light for my path." God has given us His Word to *illuminate* our lives. In this chapter we are going to take a look at three important aspects of that illumination.

Illumination's Source

A few years ago, the elders of our church were wrestling with a difficult situation. One of them mentioned a passage in the gospel of Matthew that he thought might be relevant to our discussion. We all turned to that text to take a closer look at it. But after we read the verses together, we weren't quite sure how to interpret them correctly. No problem. I just pulled a commentary on Matthew's Gospel off my shelf (a book of several hundred pages, written by a Bible scholar) and read aloud what it had to say about our passage. Unfortunately, we didn't understand what the *commentary* had to say about the passage in Matthew that we didn't understand. (Understand?)

Now what? Fortunately, the New Testament expert who had written that Matthew commentary is a friend of mine. He was one of my professors in graduate school. So I called him up. And I asked him for an explanation of his commentary's explanation of our passage. We had a very enlightening conversation, after which I was able to guide our elders in applying an important principle from Matthew to our difficult situation.

Now, wouldn't *you* love to have the phone number of your very own Bible scholar/friend on speed dial? When you're reading the Bible this week and come across something you don't understand, you could just punch that number and Bob-the-Bible-Brain would pick up. Then you could ask him: "What's the deal with all those funky dietary laws that Moses recorded in Leviticus?" Or, "What does Paul mean by 'justification' in Romans 3?" Imagine having your very own Bible scholar/friend—just a phone call away.

Hey, I've got an even crazier idea! Instead of calling some modern-day Bible scholar, what if you could text your question to the *original* author of any portion of Scripture? What if you could contact Moses *directly* about those funky dietary laws in Leviticus, or ask the apostle Paul *himself* to explain justification in Romans 3 to you?

OK. I'll go one better than that—better than a modern-day Bible scholar at your service, better than a direct connection with one of the Bible's original authors. What if God Himself—who inspired those original human authors to write what they wrote—were available to explain Bible passages to you? Cool!

Well, I'm not making up this last option. Look at what the apostle Paul wrote to the Corinthians about God's assistance in illuminating our understanding of what He's communicated to us:

For who among men knows the thoughts of a man except the man's spirit within him? In the same way no one knows the thoughts of God except the Spirit of God. We have not received the spirit of the world but the Spirit who is from God, that we may understand what God has freely given us. This is what we speak, not in words taught us by human wisdom but in words taught by the Spirit, expressing spiritual truths in spiritual words. The man without the Spirit does not accept the things that come from the Spirit of God, for they are foolishness to him, and he cannot understand them, because they are spiritually discerned. (1 Corinthians 2:11–14)

Now, there's a ton of stuff in these verses that I would love to unpack—but I'm only going to take the time to explain the basic flow of what the apostle Paul is teaching here. First, Paul points out that nobody knows or understands God quite like God's own Spirit (verse 11: "No one knows the thoughts of God except the Spirit of God").

Second, Paul reminds his readers that, if they're now Christ followers, they have God's Spirit living on the inside. This is one of the benefits that Jesus promises those who surrender their lives to Him. When you ask Jesus to forgive your sins and rule your life, He gives you the Holy Spirit as a signing bonus (verse 12: "We have not received the spirit of the world but the Spirit who is from God").

Third, Paul explains that this is the reason that some people understand the things that come from God (e.g., the Bible) and other people don't. If you've begun to follow Jesus and have God's Spirit on the inside, God's Spirit helps you understand God's Word. On the other hand, if you're not yet a Christ follower, then the Holy Spirit doesn't indwell you and it's not surprising that you find the Bible to be confusing, boring, unrelated to your life, or just plain not worth reading.

This means that if you want God's Word to shine light on your path, you first need the Holy Spirit to shine light on God's Word. (That last sentence is so important that I'm going to ask you to go back and read it a second time. Thanks.) Theologians have a name for the truth that I'm describing here. They call it the *doctrine of illumination.* God wants to speak to you. He speaks through His Word, the Bible. But you won't be able to make sense of what God's saying until you surrender your life to Christ and the Holy Spirit comes to live in you. Have you done that yet?

YOU CANNOT make sense of what God's saying until you surrender your life to Christ and the Holy Spirit comes to live in you.

Now, please don't misunderstand me here. You don't need the Holy Spirit in order to make sense of the Bible from an *external* standpoint. Anybody can read a Bible and understand it externally. Anybody can follow the meaning of its words, or the structure of its sentences, or the logic of its passages. However, as Martin Luther, the great reformer and theologian of the sixteenth century, put it: there's a big difference between the *external* clarity of the Bible, which anybody can grasp, and the *internal* clarity of the Bible—what it means for our lives personally—which only those with God's Spirit on the inside can grasp. (I haven't been able to track down where Luther said this. But trust me—I'm sure he said it.)

And only when you are able to grasp God's Word does it begin to grasp you. Are you experiencing this? When you read the Bible, do things jump off the page at you? Do you get excited as you come across truths that have direct bearing on your life? That's God's Spirit *illuminating* the text for you.

In fact, every time you pick up your Bible to read it, or study it in a small group, or listen to it in a sermon, it's a good idea to offer a quick prayer: *God, may Your Spirit help me understand and apply to my life what I'm about to encounter in Your Word.* I can't emphasize strongly enough how important it is to approach God's Word by prayerfully inviting the Spirit to speak to you. If you're a Christ follower, the Holy Spirit is now your internal tutor.

Of course, this doesn't mean that everything you come across in the Bible is going to be easy to understand. Yes, the

Holy Spirit is going to help you. But like any good teacher who uses an assortment of pedagogical tools to get the job done (e.g., visual aids, textbooks, lab experiments), the Spirit uses a variety of means to help you understand and apply the Bible to your life: a study Bible, a good small group curriculum, the teaching pastors of your church, and so on. But you will still be amazed—once you have the Holy Spirit on the inside—at how much of the Bible comes alive to you with no outside help.

THE UNDERLYING source of all biblical understanding is the Holy Spirit. He is what you need most.

You may have been raised in a church tradition where you were taught *not* to study the Bible on your own. Without the assistance of a priest, or a minister, or a rabbi—you were warned—you would not be able to make sense of the Bible. While I would certainly agree that gifted teachers are a tremendous asset when it comes to gaining insight from God's Word, let me repeat my point that the underlying source of all biblical understanding is the Holy Spirit. He is what you need most. And if you have Him, a good portion of the Bible is going to be clear to you without any additional input.

Theologians call this the *doctrine of perspicuity.* (It's closely related to the *doctrine of illumination,* which I mentioned earlier.) I'll bet you don't know what *perspicuity* means. Give up? It means *clarity*. You gotta love theologians—they choose an obscure word like *perspicuity* to talk about clarity.

The *doctrine of perspicuity* expresses a great truth. Here it is (in my own words): God's Word will be clear, for the most part, to those who have put their trust in Jesus Christ. Why? Because the Spirit, as your resident tutor, will illuminate the Bible (see John 14:26; 16:13–15). And once the Spirit begins to illuminate the Bible for you, the Bible will be able to illuminate your life. You will discover, as the psalmist did, that God's Word is "a lamp to [your] feet and a light for [your] path" (Psalm 119:105).

Illumination's Condition

Let me tell you an Old Testament story about a guy named Naaman. (You can find it in 2 Kings 5 if you want to read it for yourself.) Naaman was the commander of the king's army in Aram, one of Israel's adversaries. The Bible describes him as "a great man in the sight of his master and . . . a valiant soldier" (v. 1). But in spite of all that Naaman had going for him, he had one horrific problem: *leprosy*. Leprosy was an incurable disease that could take his life.

As God would have it, in Naaman's household there was a Jewish servant girl who was familiar with the miracle-working ministry of an Israeli prophet named Elisha. When the servant girl told her master about this potential source of healing, Naaman pulled together some money, got a letter of recommendation from his king, and made a beeline for Israel.

Arriving at Elisha's home and expecting to be personally welcomed by the prophet, Naaman was a tad insulted when a servant was sent to the door to greet him. And what was worse—the servant delivered these bizarre instructions to Naaman: "Go, wash yourself seven times in the Jordan, and your flesh will be restored" (v. 10). Well, Naaman was a proud man and the Jordan River was a dirty and unimpressive stream, so he rejected Elisha's secondhand counsel. There was no way that he was going to obey this humiliating directive. Naaman revved up his chariot and prepared to return home to Aram.

But Naaman's servants wouldn't let their boss throw in the towel. They said (my paraphrase of verse 13): "Yeah, it looks like a stupid command—dunk in the Jordan River seven times. But what harm would it do to give it a try?" So Naaman gave it a try. And he came out of the water completely cleansed of his leprosy.

Here's the point that I want to draw out of this story. As long as Naaman refused to heed Elisha's instructions, those instructions had zero impact on his life. In fact, those instructions seemed ridiculous (unreasonable, absurd, preposterous) to him. But once Naaman made up his mind to *obey* the words of

God's prophet, those instructions changed his life. It will work the same way in your life. Only when you come to the Bible with a submissive attitude will the Bible truly impact you.

ONLY WHEN you come to the Bible with a submissive attitude will the Bible truly impact you.

If you approach the Bible with an unsubmissive attitude, not only will you gain nothing from it, you may even conclude that some of its instructions are just plain stupid. So illumination's condition is a submissive attitude. God's Word is not going to make sense to you until you approach it with a willingness to do what it says. The Holy Spirit is eager to illuminate the Bible for those who are eager to obey it. Note the close connection between illumination and obedience in the following passage:

> Jesus replied, "If anyone loves me, he will obey my teaching. My Father will love him, and we will come to him and make our home with him. He who does not love me will not obey my teaching. These words you hear are not my own; they belong to the Father who sent me.
>
> "All this I have spoken while still with you. But the Counselor, the Holy Spirit, whom the Father will send in my name, will teach you all things and will remind you of everything I have said to you." (John 14:23–26)

One of the Bible interpretation rules presented in *Context* is to look for repeating words or ideas. Three very significant words pop up several times in this little clump of verses you just read. Can you pick them out? One of them is "teaching" (or "teach"). Jesus is pointing out something that we already noted in 1 Corinthians 2: the Holy Spirit has been given to Christ followers as an internal *Teacher.* He is *illumination's source.* One of His jobs is to help us understand God's Word.

What are the other two repeating words in this passage? *Love* and *obey.* If we expect the Holy Spirit's teaching to make sense to us and impact our lives, then we need to approach God's Word in an attitude of loving obedience. That's the condition for receiving illumination.

Let me illustrate the importance of meeting this condition with something Jesus said to a group of His detractors who failed in this regard: "You diligently study the Scriptures because you think that by them you possess eternal life. These are the Scriptures that testify about me, yet you refuse to come to me to have life" (John 5:39–40).

Do you follow Jesus' accusation here? He's telling a bunch of religious leaders that they don't "get" God's Word. Specifically, they don't grasp what the Bible has to say about eternal life. Why not? Well, it wasn't because they hadn't studied the Bible. They were Bible experts! No, the problem was that they didn't meet the *condition* for Bible illumination. What's the condition? You've got to approach the Bible with a submissive attitude—with a willingness to obey whatever it says. The religious leaders didn't meet that condition, as demonstrated by the fact that they refused to come to Jesus for eternal life even though that's exactly what the Bible instructed them to do!

What about *you*? What disposition do you bring to the Bible? Do you approach the Bible like it's an all-you-can-eat buffet, where you are free to take what you want and leave the rest? Don't expect the Holy Spirit to illuminate God's Word and God's Word to light your path if *that's* your attitude. In fact, I'd encourage you to confess any such attitude to God as sin. Tell God you're sorry for the arrogance of picking and choosing which parts of the Bible you're going to obey. Ask Him to forgive you, and to give you a submissive, eager-to-obey-everything-He-says spirit.

A number of years ago, I attended a pastors' conference at a well-known megachurch in California. In fact, the church had recently been in the news. A large group of pro-choice protestors had picketed one Sunday morning because the church had a reputation for teaching a pro-life position.

News reporters and camera crews from nearby Los Angeles TV stations were recording the action. The senior pastor told us of one reporter's comment and subsequent conversation. The TV reporter had stuck a microphone in the pastor's face and said,

"I must admit that I've been a little surprised by your church. I wasn't familiar with it before today, so when I heard that you were being picketed by a pro-choice group, I just imagined a different sort of church than the one I've found."

The pastor politely asked, "What sort of church did you imagine?"

"Well, I'll tell you what I *didn't* imagine," the reporter replied. "I *didn't* imagine a church that would have so many attenders. Why, even the local mayor goes here . . . and lots of young, well-educated women! How did you manage to get so many people to buy into a pro-life position?" (There's no such thing as media bias, right?)

Here was the pastor's explanation. He said (my paraphrase): "The issue is not getting people to buy into a pro-life position. The issue is getting people to submit to the authority of God's Word. Because once they are willing to do whatever God says, then all we have to do is teach them what God says and they're eager to obey it. So, if the Bible says that God knits a baby together in its mother's womb before the child is ever born [Psalm 139], then our church's members are going to protect that unborn baby!"

Did you follow that? You must choose between two approaches to the Bible. Either God's Word is going to stand in authority over you (i.e., you're willing to obey whatever it says), or you are going to stand in authority over God's Word (i.e., you'll pick and choose what you want to obey).

Let me encourage you to go with the first of those two positions. Determine that you

EITHER GOD'S Word is going to stand in authority over you, or you are going to stand in authority over God's Word.

will submit to the authority of God's Word. Only then will God's Spirit illuminate the Bible for you. And only then will the Bible illuminate your life.

Beware of any traces of an unsubmissive attitude—any tendencies to dismiss the Bible's directives as outdated, or ridiculous, or not worthy of serious consideration. Watch for rebellious thoughts. The Bible on sexual purity? *Nobody follows those standards anymore!* The Bible on tithing? *Who'd be crazy enough to give 10 percent of their paycheck to the church?* The Bible on forgiving those who abuse you? *You don't know my boss!* The Bible on training your children in Scripture? *When is there time to do that between sports and music lessons and family getaways?*

Keep in mind that *illumination's condition* is a submissive attitude.

Illumination's Aim

We're about to take a look at one of the word pictures the Bible uses to describe itself. But before we look at this word picture in the epistle of James, let me mention several other Bible metaphors that appear throughout Scripture. Significantly, they all describe the Bible as something that's very active, very dynamic. The Bible is not just a book that's intended to sit on a shelf or coffee table or kitchen counter gathering dust. It's God's means of accomplishing His purposes in our lives.

Psalm 119:105 describes God's Word as a lamp that lights our path. Jeremiah 23:29 depicts it as both a fire that purifies and a hammer that breaks up the hardness of our heart. Ephesians 6:17 calls it a sword that we're to use when fighting our spiritual enemies. First Peter 2:2 portrays it as milk that nourishes us. And James 1:21 paints it as a seed that sprouts to eternal life in us.

You get the idea. God intends the Bible to work us over. God's Word is meant to do something *to* us, or *in* us, or *for* us.

GOD'S WORD is meant to do something *to* us, or *in* us, or *for* us.

Now let's look at the word picture in James:

Do not merely listen to the word, and so deceive yourselves. Do what it says. Anyone who listens to the word but does not do what it says is like a man who looks at his face in a mirror and, after looking at himself, goes away and immediately forgets what he looks like. But the man who looks intently into the perfect law that gives freedom, and continues to do this, not forgetting what he has heard, but doing it—he will be blessed in what he does. (James 1:22–25)

What metaphor is used to describe the Bible in these verses? *A mirror.* How can we use the Bible like a mirror in our lives? Well, there are a couple of ways to look into a mirror. The first is to cast a quick glance into it as you're walking by. You might wink at yourself, or smile . . . but that's about it. The other way is to gaze intently into the mirror in order to make some adjustment to yourself. You comb your hair, or shave your face, or pick the spinach leaf from between your teeth, or practice the hand gestures for your presentation at school or work, or evaluate how many pounds you have to lose, or try on a new outfit. Whatever. You look into the mirror with the *aim* of improving yourself.

In a similar fashion, there are two ways of looking into God's Word. The first is to look into it and do *nothing*. The other way is to look into it and do *something*. James says that we should always look into the Bible with the aim of doing *something*—making some God-pleasing improvement to our lives. The final goal of reading or studying or listening to a sermon from the Bible is not *knowledge*. It's *life-change*. Gaining

Bible knowledge is important, but only as a means to an end. The end is to do something with what we've just learned.

I am constantly promoting Community Groups (small group Bible studies) at our church. I love to see men, women, and students commit to a weekly venue where they'll dig into God's Word with friends. But surprisingly, I also do a fair amount of talking people *out* of Community Groups. Why would I talk somebody out of Bible study? Because I frequently run into people who are in multiple groups. Now, I suppose that on rare occasions it's beneficial to be in *two* groups at once (especially if you're married, and one of the groups is a couples group). But I get concerned when people confuse Bible *knowledge* (learning lots of "deep" Bible factoids in multiple groups) with Bible *life transformation* (putting what's been learned into practice).

One of my constant mantras is: *It's not how much of the Bible you get through that matters, but how much of the Bible gets through you!* If you're taking in more Scripture than you can put into practice, it would be better to scale back to one small group meeting and to focus on *walking* the Word. The same goes for the amount of Bible you import through Christian radio and the sermon podcasts of your favorite communicator. The aim of being illuminated by God's Word is to *apply what you've learned* to your life.

My best buddy in college was the wide receiver on the

football team. One day I was talking to him about the upcoming NFL playoffs—what teams I thought would win, who my favorite players were . . . that kind of stuff. Suddenly it dawned on me that this guy wasn't participating in the conversation. In fact,

DON'T SETTLE for merely reading the Bible or studying it or listening to it preached. Put the Bible into play in your life.

he didn't seem to know very much about the National Football League. So I gave him a hard time. "You're a football player and yet you hardly know anything about professional football!" He quickly retorted: "I'd rather *play* football than *watch* it!"

He's right. Participating beats observing. Don't settle for "watching" the Bible—merely reading it, or studying it, or listening to it preached. Put the Bible into play in your life. Let it always be your *aim* to come away from God's Word with an application for your life. You could even do that right now with something you learned in this chapter about *Illumination's Source* (the Holy Spirit), *Illumination's Condition* (a submissive, eager-to-obey attitude), and *Illumination's Aim* (to put something into practice). What's your application?

Perhaps you're thinking: *I'm not sure how to craft good applications from what I learn in the Bible. How do I go from text to life?* Good question. That's what we're going to cover in the next chapter.

Study Guide

The *Study Guide* questions at the end of each chapter have been designed for your personal benefit. *All* questions can be used for personal study and, if you're part of a discussion group, for preparation for your group meeting. If you are part of a small group, you will find that the questions preceded by the group icon ( ) are especially useful for discussion. Your group leader can choose from among those questions when the group meets.

Icebreakers

- Describe a time in your life when you were caught in the dark—without a light.

- When you read the Bible on your own, how often do you come away from it with a specific application for your life? (Explain your answer.)

    Always

    Frequently

    Sometimes

    Seldom

1. If a person regularly finds the Bible to be confusing, boring, or difficult to apply to their life, what might that indicate? Why?

2. Read Ephesians 1:13–14. How does a person get the Holy Spirit? What picture does Paul paint in these verses about the Holy Spirit's role in the lives of believers? Why should this be encouraging to a Christ follower?

3. (•••) Read 1 Corinthians 2:11–14 and Romans 8:5–17. Make a list of ways in which the Holy Spirit demonstrates His presence in a person's life. Circle the evidences on the list that you see in your own life.

4. What do you learn in John 14:15–17, 26 and John 16:7–15 about the Holy Spirit's role as your personal Bible teacher?

(•••) If the Holy Spirit has been given to you as a resident tutor, how might that impact the way in which you approach reading, studying, and applying the Bible?

5. What is the *condition* you must meet in order for the Holy Spirit to illuminate God's Word for you? What might be some indications of such an attitude on your part?

6. (icon) What has been one or two of the hardest lessons for you to learn from God's Word? Why were they so difficult to apply?

7. What does Paul warn us *not* to do to the Holy Spirit in Ephesians 4:30? Read the surrounding context to this verse (vv. 25–32) and note the sorts of behaviors that would do this to God's Spirit.

(icon) How might grieving the Holy Spirit affect His role as your teacher and illuminator of God's Word?

8. (icon) Explain how the Bible serves as a mirror in the life of a Christ follower.

What are some tips for using the Bible as a mirror that you pick up in James 1:22–25?

In the very next verses (James 1:26–27), what are some of the changes that James says should be made in our lives after looking into the mirror of God's Word?

9. (icon) What is something you will *start* doing or *stop* doing as an application of this chapter?

{ 2 }

From Text to Life

MY TWENTY-FIVE-YEAR-OLD son, Andrew, is a Pied Piper when it comes to younger kids. Children love to hang out with him. He's a good time. So it didn't surprise me when Andrew, after graduating from college, landed a job as a sixth-grade teacher. Nor was I surprised when he turned out to be one of the most popular teachers in the school. Not many teachers would take on thirty kids in a game of playground dodge ball! But this became a favorite pastime of Andrew, along with engaging students in personal conversations and making English literature cool.

As Andrew began his first summer break as a teacher, he decided to make some extra income by offering to tutor students. A few of his own kids were immediately interested. So were a couple of their friends from other schools. But Andrew quickly noticed a big difference between his own kids and their outside friends. His own kids were used to his interactive teaching style. He'd trained them to contribute to lively discussions.

This wasn't the case with their outside friends. Andrew was incredulous when he asked one young girl some questions about her reading assignment and her eyes glazed over. She didn't have an answer. This was new territory for him.

As he was telling me this story, he said, "She just looked at me, Dad. She just looked at me! I could tell she hadn't read her assignment very thoroughly—because she had nothing to say."

Maybe you feel like that little girl when you read the Bible. Maybe you have a hard time paying attention. Maybe you don't get anything out of it. Maybe your eyes glaze over. Maybe you're not reading the Bible with any regularity . . . because you're just not drawn to it. In the last chapter I cautioned that if this is true of you, it could be an indication that you don't yet have a personal relationship with Jesus Christ. Because once you begin a relationship with Jesus, the first thing He does is give you the Holy Spirit. God's Spirit comes to live inside of you. And one of the Spirit's jobs is to make God's Word come alive to you. He gives you a love for the Bible and helps you understand it and apply it to your life.

So if you are not experiencing this yourself, it *could* be that the Holy Spirit isn't presently living on the inside. You need to surrender your life to Christ. That's *one* possibility. Another possibility is that the Holy Spirit *does* live in you, but you've just never been taught how to put the Bible into practice. You'd really like to be able to do this, but it seems like a daunting task. The reason your eyes glaze over is *not* because you're disinterested in the Bible; they glaze over because you don't know how to *walk* the Word. You don't know how to move *from text to life.*

This chapter will offer you a step-by-step process for doing that—four steps in all. And you're not going to forget these four points, because I'm going to give them to you in the form of an acronym. Taken together, the first letter of each step spells a word: *COMA.* Follow these instructions and you'll break out of a spiritual *coma* as you read the Bible. Instead of your eyes glazing over, you'll sense God prompting and empowering you to *do* something. (Just for the record, the COMA acronym is not original with me. I don't know who first came up with it, but it's been used by Christ followers for years as a reminder of how the Bible application process works. I just like COMA because it's memorable.)

C: Context

When you're reading a passage from the Bible, before you can apply that passage to your *own* life, you need to understand what it meant to its original audience. What was their *context*?

Let me illustrate why context is so important. Stephen Covey, author of the bestselling book *The 7 Habits of Highly Effective People*, tells the story about a time he was riding a train in the city. There was a father on the train with three young kids—and those kids were really acting up. They were running up and down the aisle, banging into people. And the dad just sat there, oblivious to the havoc his children were causing.

Finally, Covey couldn't take it any longer. He tapped the dad on the shoulder and said, "Sir, your children are really disturbing a lot of people. I wonder if you couldn't control them a little more?" The dad looked up and replied, "Oh, you're right. I guess I should do something about it. We just came from the hospital where their mother died about an hour ago. I don't know what to think, and I guess they don't know how to handle it either." Covey immediately felt like a total jerk. He had jumped to the wrong conclusion because he hadn't taken the time to understand this dad's context. And so Covey warns us, in his book, not to make the same mistake. Don't read your autobiography into other people's lives.[1]

That's good advice to follow when you're reading the Bible. Don't try to figure out what God is saying to *you* until you've figured out what God was saying to the original audience. What was the context of that audience? We covered this topic in detail in book three of the Bible Savvy series (*Context*), which dealt with the rules of Bible interpretation. The basic premise behind these rules is: *You must understand the context.*

And there are four contexts that you need to consider for

every Bible passage. The first is the passage's *historical setting.* Who wrote the book of the Bible that you're reading? Who were they writing to? When did the action in this book take place? (1400 BC? AD 60?) What was going on in the world at the time? What problem was the author addressing in the lives of his readers? You can easily acquire this information by reading the brief introduction to any Bible book in your study Bible.

Second, you need to consider your passage's *literary setting.* There are at least six different kinds of literature in the Bible, and different rules for interpreting each one. You don't interpret, for example, an Old Testament law in the same way that you interpret one of David's psalms—or a prophecy in Isaiah, or a parable in Matthew's Gospel, or a directive in one of Paul's epistles. Let me remind you of why the rules of interpreting these various genres are so important by relating an amusing anecdote.

Several years ago, a guy wrote a bestseller called *The Year of Living Biblically.* The author decided that he would try to obey all the Old Testament laws for an entire year. Now, if you read *Context,* you may recall that one of the rules for interpreting Old Testament laws is to differentiate between laws that were only meant for ancient Israel and laws that are still in force today. Well, this guy obviously didn't know about that rule. He tried to obey *all* the laws—from not cursing others to not shaving his beard. (The not-shaving-the-beard law turned out to be a real bummer, because his beard itched like crazy and it kept getting him stopped at airport security checkpoints.)

But the funniest story this guy told was about the time he met a man in the park, who asked him why he was dressed so strange. He told the man that he was trying to obey all the Old Testament laws—from dressing a certain way, to stoning adulterers. The man became indignant. He admitted, "I cheated on my wife years ago. So are you going to stone me?" Well, the author of the book was prepared for a scenario like this. He reached into his pocket and took out a handful of pebbles and began to toss them at the adulterer. The adulterer was not amused. He grabbed the pebbles from the author's hand and began throwing them back.[2]

A passage's *literary setting* is important. It helps if you know the rules for interpreting laws or prophecies or narratives or proverbs or whatever. (For a detailed discussion of the literary setting, see chapter 2 of *Context*.)

"ASK AND IT will be given to you" doesn't mean that you can pray to win the lottery and God will grant your request.

Third, you must consider your passage's *theological setting.* Consider what the *whole* Bible teaches about whatever topic you come across in the passage that you happen to be reading. In *Context*, we explored the topic of prayer along these lines. Just because you read in Matthew 7:7, "Ask and it will be given to you," doesn't mean that you can pray to win the lottery and God will grant your request. No, the Bible has more to say about prayer than what you find in Matthew 7:7. Whatever topic you come across in a Bible passage—don't jump to any conclusions about that topic until you've considered what the rest of the Bible has to say about it.

Fourth, look at a passage's *immediate setting*. Don't view a Bible word in isolation. How does that word fit into the sentence you found it in? How does that sentence fit into its host paragraph? How does that paragraph fit into the surrounding chapter, and that chapter into the book of the Bible that you're reading?

Before you can apply a Bible passage to your own life, you must understand what it meant to its original audience. What are the *historical, literary, theological,* and *immediate settings* of your passage? Don't be overwhelmed by this assignment. Much of the information you're looking for, as I've repeatedly said, can be culled from the book introductions and the page footnotes of a good study Bible.

O: Observations

Once you've scoped out the *context* of the Bible passage that you're about to dive into, your next step is to read the passage and make as many *observations* about it as you possibly can.

A couple of months ago, I was working out at the health club and I began talking about books with one of the guys I had met there. Gary, a corporate attorney, loves to read mystery novels. Recently, he'd been reading Erle Stanley Gardner mysteries—the author who wrote the stories that the old *Perry Mason* TV series was based on. When he finished the books, he went to the library and checked out the black-and-white DVDs of that series.

Soon Gary had me hooked on *Perry Mason*. It took a little bit of work to get into a dated courtroom drama, but it eventually grabbed me. Maybe it was the '58 Ford T-Bird that Perry drove around in. Whatever, this crime-solving lawyer taught me how to look for clues in a murder mystery. As I watched each episode, trying to beat Perry to the punch, I got better and better at making astute observations.

That's what you want to do when you read a passage in the Bible. You want to make insightful *observations*. What should you be looking for? Let me suggest four things to keep your eyes open for: *the theme, repeating words or ideas, something striking*, and *truths about God*.

Theme. If you had to summarize the passage you just read in a word or phrase, what would it be? Is this passage about: *Jesus' power to do miracles? How to resolve conflicts? The sins of Moab and Edom? God's help in trouble?* What's the theme of the passage? If you've got a study Bible, you might want to note what it calls the passage you've just read. Your Bible gives every section a title.

Just a word of clarification here: If you sit down and read an entire chapter from the Bible, that chapter may contain multiple themes. For example, if you're reading one of the New Testament Gospels, one chapter may recount three different episodes from a day in the life of Jesus (each with its own theme), or four different parables that Jesus tells. If you're reading a chapter from the book of Proverbs, there may be a dozen or more different themes in that single chapter.

AN ENTIRE chapter from the Bible may contain multiple themes.

What should you do when your passage contains multiple themes? Well, if your end goal is to make an application from that text to your personal life, just choose *one* of the themes to work with. Which theme are you drawn to? Each theme will have its own application. You need to focus on one of them.

Repeating Words or Ideas. If God repeats the same word or idea in a chapter, you can count on the fact that He wants you to pay attention to it. This past week, as I was following my daily Bible reading schedule, I found myself in First

Timothy. In chapter 2 of that epistle, Paul talks about the importance of *prayer* several times. *Aha!* I thought: *God's got something to say to me about prayer.* That's how it's done. Keep your eyes open for repeating words or ideas. Circle them in your Bible. Draw a line between them, connecting them.

Something Striking. I'm not always sure why certain things jump out at me when I'm reading the Bible—but they do. That'll happen to you, too. Something may strike you because it's unexpected. Or maybe it's something you never knew before. Perhaps it catches your attention because it's strange (like, *Why did the prophet Elisha make that axhead float?*). Sometimes it addresses a problem you're currently facing or puts a finger on a sin you've recently been guilty of.

If a line or a verse in a chapter strikes you—for whatever reason—underline it, or put an exclamation point in the margin next to it. A couple of weeks ago, my Bible reading schedule took me to the book of Second Samuel. I read an entire chapter that listed the names of King David's key fighting men. My first reaction was: *Not a lot in this chapter to apply to my life today.* But then something struck me. The chapter noted that among the hundreds of warriors that followed David, there was a special group referred to as The Thirty. Not only that, there was a select group within The Thirty who were called The Three.

Here's the observation that popped into my head: *David*

focused his attention on a handful of guys that he gave extra time and attention to. And then I recalled that Jesus did the same thing, right? The Gospels tell us that Jesus had seventy committed followers, and twelve disciples within that group of seventy. Finally, within those twelve were three guys (Peter, James, and John) with whom He was especially close.

Wow! It was really helpful to make that observation in Second Samuel. I'm glad I noted something that struck me. (I'll come back to this in a moment.)

Truths about God. This is always a good observation to make. Whatever passage you read in the Bible—what does it tell you about God? If the Bible is revelation from God about God and His plans, then many Bible passages will be telling you and me truths about God. Mark them down in your Bible's margins (or personal notebook or journal) when you see them. Note any attributes that describe what God is like, or any actions that recount what God has done.

So when it comes to observations, look for themes, repeating words or ideas, something striking, and truths about God. Now let's go back to COMA: C stands for *Context.* O stands for *Observations.* M stands for . . .

M: Message

What is the basic *message* that God wants to communicate to you through the passage you're reading? Before you can answer this question, you *must* complete the first two steps of COMA. You must consider the passage's context and make as many observations about the passage as possible. The *context* and the *observations* steps will help you understand what the passage meant to its original audience. What was God saying to *them?* Until you know the answer to that question, you're not ready to determine what God is saying to *you.* You're liable to read into the text something that isn't there. You'll read your autobiography into it.

So the C and the O steps of COMA focus on the original audience. But the *M* and the *A* steps shift the focus to you. *M* stands for *message.* What is the basic message that God seems to be communicating through this passage? This message will come out of one of your observations.

What happens if you make multiple observations? Suppose you read a chapter in the book of Acts and note three different themes, four repeating words, two things that really strike you, and one big truth about God. Just choose *one* of these observations to work with—whichever one you feel most drawn to. (Hopefully, the Holy Spirit will be influencing this decision, because He knows exactly what you need to get out of the Bible on any given day.) This observation will lead to the specific message that you are about to take away from the text.

Let me say it again: The message you draw from your daily

dose of the Bible will be based on *one* of the observations you make while reading your passage. Let me show you how this works. Earlier, under "Observations," I mentioned that while reading a chapter in Second Samuel I was struck by the fact that David had a special group of followers called The Thirty, and a subset within that group called The Three. That was my observation. What message might I draw from such an observation? Here's the one that occurred to me: "No leader can mentor everybody. So good leaders pour time and attention into a handful of followers."

Do you see how I did that? When you're drawing a message out of one of your observations, try to construct that message in the form of a timeless principle. What I mean by a timeless principle is a lesson that can be applied to everyone who ever reads that text. It's the sort of thing that could be stated on a wall plaque. "Good leaders pour time and attention into a handful of followers." Wouldn't that make a catchy saying for a wall plaque or a great caption for a leadership poster?

If you have a hard time *seeing* a timeless principle behind one of your observations, it may help to put on your SPECS. SPECS is another acronym (as well as a nickname for spectacles or glasses). Now, I don't want to confuse you by piling up acronyms in this chapter, but I think you'll find SPECS to be very useful. (Like COMA, I have no idea who to credit for coming up with it. It's been around for some time.)

You put on your SPECS by asking yourself five questions. In the Bible passage do you see a:

> **S**in to confess?
> **P**romise to claim?
> **E**xample to follow?
> **C**ommand to obey?
> **S**tatement about God (i.e., some truth about who He is or what He's done)?

Those are your SPECS!

Let's go back to my observation in Second Samuel about David and his groups of The Thirty and The Three. Which letter of SPECS did I use to get a message out of that observation? *E*: an *example* to follow. David modeled a wonderful leadership strategy that I should adopt: "Good leaders pour time and attention into a handful of followers."

One final thought about getting a message out of the text. This is something creative for you to consider doing (and it's strictly extra credit for overachievers). See if you can capture your message (timeless principle) in the form of a pithy title. If you were going to write a book or preach a sermon on your message, what would you call it? Here's what I titled the message on leadership that I drew out of Second Samuel: *My Guys*. A bit trite? Perhaps, but *My Guys* captured the essence of the message that God's Word spoke to me. That title stuck in my mind as a reminder to identify a few men in whose lives I might make a significant investment.

I do this, by the way, every time I read the Bible. I give a title to the message that I've drawn out of an observation from the passage. I taught my kids how to do that during family devotions as they were growing up. I also taught the guys in my Community Group how to do it. And now I've taught *you* how to do it. You'll find it to be a creative and memorable way to sum up the message you take away from a passage.

A: Application

The application is where the rubber meets the road. This is where you come away with something to put into practice. This is where you actually begin to *walk* the Word. Let me give you three couplets that can help to make this happen. They all start with the letter *P* so they'll be easier to remember (and because the preacher in me can't resist the urge to alliterate on occasion).

Personal and Specific. It's time to take that message (timeless principle) you came up with—the one that applies to everybody—and bring it home to your own life. Let's say, for example, that you've just read a Bible passage that emphasizes the importance of prayer. The message you drew out of the text was: *Prayer is important.* Great! What are you going to do about it? You reply: "I need to pray more." Wonderful! That's *personal*. But it's not *specific*. And applications that lack specificity are seldom put into practice. When are you going to pray more? You decide: "I'm going to get up ten minutes earlier each day and spend that extra time before work in prayer." Much better! That's both *personal and specific*.

Let me give you something harder to apply to your life. Let's say that you've just read a Bible passage and one of the observations that you made was: *God is merciful.* (This is one of those *truths about God* that you're keeping an eye out for.) A terrific observation! But observation is only the second step in the COMA process. What's the third step—the *M*? Is there a message (timeless principle) to be drawn from the observation that *God is merciful?*

You could probably come up with several messages. *Because God is merciful, He forgives sins. Because God is merciful to us, He expects us to be merciful to others. Because God is merciful, He is worthy of our praise.* Those are all messages that could be drawn from the observation that *God is merciful.* But they're not yet applications—because they're not yet *personal and specific*.

Take the first message: *Because God is merciful, He forgives sins.* How could you make that personal and specific? You could say: "I'm going to take time to confess my sins right now and ask God to forgive me." And then you do it. Or, take the second message: *Because God is merciful to us, He expects us to be merciful to others.* A great message—put it on a wall plaque—but it's not yet an application. Make it personal and specific: "Today, I am going to extend mercy to Jason (or Tammy or Adam or some other person who's offended me), because God has extended mercy to me."

What if you had come up with the third message? *Because God is merciful, He is worthy of our praise.* That's so

A MESSAGE becomes an application when you make it personal and specific.

true! But it's not *personal and specific.* How could you praise God for His mercy in a way that's personal and specific? You could sing along with a worship CD on your way to work. You could tell three people about how God has been merciful to you. You could make a list of all the ways that God has shown you mercy. Those are true applications.

Paper and Pen. Write out your application. You won't come up with a definitive application unless you write something down. Really, you won't! At best, you'll come away from your Bible reading with an ambiguous insight. But you won't actually put something into practice, because you haven't explicitly stated what that something would be.

Write out your application. Go to Walgreens or CVS. Buy a cheapo, spiral-bound notebook or a fancy journal. And write out each application that you get from the Bible. As a matter of fact, there are several things you'll want to write out. (This is all really simple and basic.) Begin with the day's date and the text that you're reading from the Bible (e.g., "Wednesday, 8/24: Hebrews 1"). Then just summarize the O, M, and A steps of COMA for your passage (i.e., the specific *observation* that led to the timeless *message* that led to your personal *application*). This may sound like a lot of writing, but it actually adds up to about a paragraph's worth of print.

Let me illustrate how this works with the passage that I keep referring to in Second Samuel. I read that passage on June 11. So I wrote in my journal, "Saturday 6/11: II Samuel 23."

Then I spelled out my *observation* (O): "Although David had many followers, he had a special group called 'The Thirty' and a group within that group called 'The Three.'"

Next I wrote down the *message* (M) that came out of the observation: *Good leaders pour time and attention into a handful of followers.*

Finally, I wrapped up my entry with an *application* (A): "I'm going to personally mentor three guys this next year by meeting with them once a week over coffee." (I even listed the names of the three guys.)

Less than a paragraph of writing. (Oh, I almost forgot. I also put the title I'd created, "My Guys," next to "II Samuel 23" at the start of my entry. But that's it.) When you take the time to do this, it crystallizes your takeaway from God's Word. Another benefit of writing something down is that it helps you remember it. I'll bet that if you read the Bible first thing in the

WHEN YOU take the time to write it down, it crystallizes your takeaway from God's Word.

morning—before you go to school or work—and you *don't* write something down, you forget what God's Word said to you by lunchtime. Right? So grab a *paper and pen* and write out your application.

Pray and Pray. I know that this sounds obvious—but it's the part of application that I most often forget to do (which is why I'm stating it twice in this couplet). I frequently write out my observation, message, and application, but then forget to ask God to help me put it into practice. And when I forget to *pray*, what I've written down ends up being just words on a page. It never gets translated into real-life action. I don't *walk* the Word.

Well . . . you've covered a lot of ground in this chapter. Now it's time to put COMA to work. In the next chapter, you'll take a look at several Bible passages and *walk* them through the steps of *context, observations, message,* and *application.*

*To watch Jim's midpoint comments about Walk,
scan this QR code with your smartphone or go to
www.biblesavvy.com/video/#walk2.*

Study Guide

Icebreakers

- Describe the most and the least relevant courses you took in school. What made them so?
- What have been your biggest challenges in getting practical applications from the Bible for your life?

1. What does COMA stand for? Describe what is meant by each letter of this acronym.

2. What are the four kinds of *contexts* to consider when reading a Bible passage? Explain why each of these is important to consider when interpreting Scripture.

3. With the help of the introductions provided for each Bible book by your personal study Bible (or a similar tool), briefly sketch out the historical contexts for the following books:

Deuteronomy

Nehemiah

Hosea

Philemon

James

4. Read Deuteronomy 8. Make some observations about this chapter in each of the four observation categories *(theme, repeating words or ideas, something striking,* and *truths about God).*

5. What is meant by the expression "timeless principle" in describing the *message* you draw out of a passage?

What is the danger in skipping the *C* and *O* steps of COMA—and moving right to the *M*?

6. What five things will SPECS help you see when crafting a *message* from a Bible passage?

Why is it beneficial to put your *message* in the form of a pithy title?

7. (●●●) Choose one of your *observations* from Deuteronomy 8 (see above) and draw a *message* (timeless principle) from it. Next, put that *message* in the form of a title.

8. Write out the four couplet-tips for making *applications* and explain why each one is important.

9. (●●●) Craft a personal *application* based upon the *message* that you drew out of Deuteronomy 8.

10. (●●●) What was the most difficult step in COMA to get the hang of as you applied it to Deuteronomy 8? Why?

{ 3 }
Coming Out of a COMA

MY SON HAS RECENTLY BECOME a photojournalist for a missions organization. (I don't know what he'll say when he discovers that I've used him as the opening illustration for two consecutive chapters in this book. But there's an old saying about it being easier to get forgiveness than permission. So sorry, Andrew.) His ministry moves him from one foreign country to another. This past week he Skyped me from Romania.

I almost didn't connect with him because I can never remember how to use Skype when it's finally time to put it to work. Yes, it's partly because I'm technologically challenged. But in my defense let me point out that there are a lot of things I forget how to do if I don't do them with some amount of frequency.

In the last chapter, I taught you the COMA steps that will enable you to start with a Bible passage and end up with a practical application of that text to your life. What are the chances that you'll remember and use these steps? Like communicating by Skype, the chances of remembering are slim to none if you don't review and practice them. That's exactly what you're about to do in this chapter. I will walk you through COMA for a couple of passages, using different genres of biblical literature as examples. If you would like to maximize your learning from this exercise, feel free to push the pause button *before* reading my insights for each text and do your own COMA study of it. Then you can compare what you've discovered for yourself with what I've come up with.

A Quick Review of the COMA Steps

COMA is a lot easier than it looks. Honest! I've read a number of books that teach Bible study methods and I've never put them to good use because of their complexity. They're too busy. But COMA is different—at least, once you get the hang of it. Let me walk you through the steps again, explaining why each is really quite simple.

Context only has to be determined when you're beginning a new book of the Bible. Let's say, for example, that you're starting to read through the epistle of First Corinthians. I recommend (and explain why in the next chapter) that you don't cover more than one chapter per day. Since there are sixteen chapters in this New Testament letter, you will be working your way through it for the next two to three weeks. But you only have to figure out the context once. And, as I've constantly reiterated, it's already spelled out for you in the brief introduction to the book that you'll find in an

NIV Study Bible. Read about the author, the recipients, the historical setting, and the purpose of First Corinthians before you delve into chapter 1—and you won't have to do so again for another few weeks. (Unless, of course, you need to refresh your memory about these details.)

The *observations* step probably seems a bit more intimidating because I've given you four things to look out for: *theme, repeating words or ideas, something striking,* and *truths about God.* But let me say a few words about this step that will make it more manageable. It is not necessary for you to squeeze every possible observation out of each chapter you read. Just note three or four that are obvious to you—even if there are several observations in each of the four categories that could be detected if you looked long and hard enough. This is not a test for which you will be graded (in case you're worried about your GPA).

When I walk you through a couple of Bible chapters in a moment, I will go overboard in making observations—but that is only to stimulate your thinking. When I'm reading a chapter for my own benefit, I typically come away with only a handful of observations. In fact, often I won't make a single observation in one or two of the four observation categories (e.g., I may not detect a repeating word or spot some great truth about God in the text). And on occasion, I am hard-pressed to find even one observation of any kind in the entire chapter (although I usually stick with it until I do). So don't go OCD trying to get all four observations in every passage you read.

The *message* step is then built on *one* of your observations. Just *one*! Which one? That's for you to decide. I try to maintain an attitude of prayer when I'm reading God's Word, so it's not unusual for me to say out loud: "Lord, there are several things in this text that have caught my attention and which I could apply to my life. Please help me choose the one that You know I need most." And then I select the observation that seems to be pregnant with significance for me personally and I craft a message from it. I jot that message down in my journal in the form of a timeless principle—most often in one sentence. A single sentence! (Although, if you're an incurable overachiever you might recall the extra credit points you can rack up by restating your message as if it were the title of a book you're writing on the subject. That title will help the message stick in your mind throughout the course of the day.)

Finally, the *application* step requires that you get specific about how to put the message of the text into practice in your life. But once again, though there may be many ways in which you might flesh things out, you only have to articulate *one*. What could be more simple? An occasional *context*, a few *observations*, a one-sentence *message*, and a single *application*. About a paragraph of writing in your journal.

Of course, if you want something that is more complex, there are plenty of Bible study methods and tools out there to choose from. Once I heard a presentation by a Bible software company. When the rep finished explaining all that his top-of-the-line product could do, I was in awe. This resource would enable its users (for a sum of money slightly less than the purchase price of a foreign car) to trace every occurrence of a word's Hebrew root throughout the Old Testament, study dozens of commentaries on any passage in Scripture, read full-page articles on Bible-related topics, yada, yada, yada.

You can go the Bible software route if you want to. But my guess is that you'll rarely use it. And you'll feel like David in King Saul's armor when you do. David couldn't wait to shed that cumbersome suit, exchanging it for five smooth stones and a simple slingshot.

Here's why I wouldn't recommend the Bible software approach to you. First, it will deluge you with information—a bazillion times more information than you could possibly digest. And besides that, your goal should not be Bible *knowledge*, right? It's the *application* of Scripture that you're shooting for. Second, if you're like most people, you have twenty to thirty minutes a day to spend in God's Word. If half that time is taken up reading an article about the bronze basin in the temple (interesting, but probably not life changing), you will walk away from your study without a sense of having connected with God. Third, Bible software is not helpful on a desert island. OK, that's a strange way to put it, but I call it my *Desert Island Principle*. I want to equip you to draw nourishment from God's Word with nothing but a Bible (admittedly, an *NIV Study Bible*), a notebook, and a pen. If you're ever abandoned on a desert island, with no Wi-Fi available, you'll still be able to glean rich insights from Scripture (which you might want to share with Tom Hanks, if you run into him and his volleyball). And speaking of a Bible, notebook, and pen—why don't you get those out, turn to 1 Kings 16, and take fifteen or twenty minutes to complete a COMA study of this chapter. I'll wait . . .

Now, be honest . . . Did you complete your COMA? I'm aware that when most of us begin reading a chapter in a book, our goal is to complete that chapter without interruption. But allow me to point out that there is no value in finishing this present chapter unless you have gotten a handle on COMA along the way. Why did you pick up *Walk* in the first place? Wasn't it because you desire to get more out of God's Word for your daily life? I promise you that this exercise will help you accomplish your goal. So if you haven't done so, please run 1 Kings 16 through COMA on your own before reading the following.

A COMA for 1 Kings 16

Hope you enjoyed doing your own COMA. Here's mine. (Of course mine is not better than yours. It's just different. The important thing is that we both found messages and applications that impact our lives and honor our God.)

Context. The book of First Kings was originally part of a single volume that included Second Kings and First and Second Samuel. Scholars are not sure who wrote this collection, although Jewish tradition credited Jeremiah (mistakenly) as the author. These books tell the tragic story of Israel's monarchy—which, ironically, began on a high note, with the reigns of Saul, David, and Solomon. But Solomon's son split the united kingdom in two, north and south, due to his foolish leadership.

The northern country, consisting of nine and one-half tribes, continued to be called Israel. It had one wicked king after another, until God allowed Assyria to destroy Israel in 722 BC and carry many of its people into captivity. The southern country, consisting of the remaining two and one-half tribes, was called Judah. Occasionally, its succession of wicked kings would be interrupted by a godly leader who would return Judah to the Lord. But these revivals didn't last for long, so in 586 BC God allowed Babylon to demolish Judah and exile many of its citizens.

The purpose of First Kings is not to give its readers a detailed historical account of Israel's monarchy. In fact, some of the kings who reigned the longest (e.g., Omri) are barely mentioned. First Kings is focused, instead, on pointing out the close connection between Israel's welfare and the people's obedience to God. Obedience brings blessing. Disobedience brings trouble. This correlation is illustrated, especially, by the lives of Israel's kings. And it's heralded, in First Kings, by two prominent prophets—Elijah and Elisha.

You didn't need me to tell you any of the above—not if you have an *NIV Study Bible*. I just summed up a few highlights from the four-page introduction to First Kings (which, by the way, is a much longer introduction than for other Old Testament books). Now, if you have a different study Bible, that's OK. If you looked at the opening page for First Kings in your study Bible, it's likely some of this background info popped up to offer valuable context.

Observations. The *theme* of this chapter is the summary of the reigns of five wicked kings from northern Israel. I learned that from the five section headings in the chapter in my *NIV Study Bible*, which list the kings by name. (The first section heading is actually found above 1 Kings 15:33: *Baasha King of Israel*. But Baasha's story is continued in the opening verses of 1 Kings 16.) This theme is not particularly scintillating, but at least it prepares me for what I'm going to find in the chapter.

There are a number of *repeating words or ideas* in 1 Kings

16. Did you notice them as you were reading the text? They occur in several clumps. But it's worth taking the clumps apart and paying attention to a few repeating ideas in each. One of these ideas is expressed by the line: "he did evil in the eyes of the Lord" (15:34; 16:7, 19, 25, 30). Another idea that pops up in the same clumps is that Israel's wicked kings were *walking in the ways of Jeroboam*. Did you see that? And what about the recurring statement that these leaders *caused Israel to commit* similar sins by their bad example? Each of these three repeating ideas is an observation from which a message could be drawn—which I'll get to in a moment. But first, a few more observations.

Did you come across *something striking* as you read 1 Kings 16? A couple of things jumped off the page at me; they really fall into the *repeated ideas* category, since both of them occur more than once in the chapter. But I'm identifying them as *something striking* because . . . well . . . they struck me. The first is that the particular sin for which these wicked kings were notorious was *idolatry* (see vv. 13, 26, 31). Evidently, not all sins are equal. Some are especially offensive to God. Which leads me to my other striking discovery: each succeeding wicked king was worse than the previous one.

EACH OF these three repeating ideas is an observation from which a message could be drawn.

This is indicated by the word *more* in describing the latest king's level of sinning (see vv. 25, 30, 33).

Any *truths about God* in this chapter? You probably picked up some that I missed. But I'll tell you the one that really caught my attention—probably because it's also a *repeating idea* in 1 Kings 16. God gets angry. Majorly angry! Especially at idolatry (see vv. 2, 7, 13, 26, 33).

Just a quick tally of my observations: one *theme*; three *repeating words or ideas*; two *something striking*(s); and one *truth about God*—for a grand total of seven observations. There are probably numerous additional observations that

ANY TRUTHS about God? . . . God gets angry. Majorly angry! Especially at idolatry.

could be made about chapter 16. But remember—my goal is *not* to squeeze every possible observation out of the text. I'm not after quantity. Besides, seven observations are more than I typically will come up with. I outdid myself so as to stimulate your ability to spot these things.

Message. I am now ready, according to the COMA approach, to select one of my seven observations and draw a message out of it. But in order to give you a better idea of how this transition from observation to message goes, I will spell out a message for every one of my observations (with the exception of the *theme* observation).

Please note that you may have made a similar observation to one of mine. This does not guarantee, however, that we both drew the same message from that observation. Often observations lend themselves to a variety of life lessons. So, if we came up with different messages for the same observation, don't assume that you've done something wrong (or, that I have). Here are the messages (timeless principles) that I derived from my observations:

Observation: The wicked kings *did evil in the eyes of the Lord.*

Message: Our sins are never done in secret but are committed in full view of God.

Observation: The wicked kings were guilty of *walking in the ways of Jeroboam.*

Message: Bad leaders leave an indelibly bad legacy.

Observation: The wicked kings *caused Israel to commit sins* similar to their own.

Message: Sins are never strictly personal—they set a bad example for others to follow.

Observation: Idolatry is a horrible sin.

Message: Rivals to God are not to be taken lightly.

Observation: Each succeeding wicked king sinned *more* than the previous one.

Message: Unchecked sin just keeps on getting worse.

Observation: God is angered by idolatry.

Message: Recognize and remove idols or face God's discipline.

Application. As with the message, it is only necessary at this point to come up with *one* application from 1 Kings 16. This application should be built on the message (drawn from one of your observations) to which God's Spirit seems to be directing your attention. Did any of your observation-message insights elicit such a response from you? Did any of them seem especially relevant to something that's currently going on in your life? Did it possibly even get an *Ouch!* out of you? Bring that message home by determining to *do* something about it—something personal and specific.

Crafting applications from messages is more art than science, which means it's easier to describe the product than explain the process. So, allow me to describe some of the possible applications that came to my mind from the messages I drew out of 1 Kings 16 (even if I can't fully explain how I came up with them).

When I meditated on the message that *our sins are never*

done in secret but are committed in full view of God, I began to wonder if there are sins in my own life that I've been treating as if they are hidden from God. My application would be to sit quietly before the Lord for a minute or two, inviting Him to identify any unconfessed and unrenounced transgressions. Then I would pray through 1 John 1:9. (I'll let you look that one up for yourself.)

A couple of the messages that I drew out of First Kings 16 have to do with the tendency of a leader's sins to be picked up by their followers. As a dad, I can certainly vouch for this unfortunate propensity in my family. While I constantly hope that my kids follow in the steps of my good qualities, I occasionally observe that they have become imitators of my negative traits. An application along these lines would be to identify and pray about any bad-dad fruits I see growing in my children's lives. God's Spirit might even prompt me to own up to one of my contagious faults in conversation with my kids.

SOME IDOLS are lurking in my life. What are they? How can I dethrone them? My application should answer these questions.

Here's one final stab at an application from First Kings 16. Two of my messages touch on the danger of idolatry. If I define an idol as anything that gets an excessive amount of my time, energy, and affection, I am sure that there are some idols (or potential idols) lurking in my life. What are they? How can I dethrone them? My application should answer these questions—*specifically*. I might also determine to do something that would exalt God to His proper place of prominence in my heart, such as singing a worship song or lifting up a prayer of thanksgiving.

How did you do with 1 Kings 16? Are you ready to try COMA with a new text? I know, I know, you're never going to finish *Walk* at this rate. But tell yourself that it's not important to read the remaining pages of this chapter before the sun goes down. Instead, make up your mind that the rest of your reading time today will be devoted to working through another passage with the help of COMA. Grab your Bible and turn to John 5.

I will take a much more abbreviated approach in presenting my COMA musings for this new text (i.e., no more rambling commentary as with 1 Kings 16). But I hope that you will be able to follow my train of thought as I move from *context* to *observations* to *message* to *applications*. Please keep in mind, once again, that I will be noting more observations than I typically come up with (like an overzealous bird-watcher who keeps handing you his binoculars so you won't miss a single species). And I'll be drawing a message out of every observation—even though COMA requires that I choose just one observation to convert into a poignant message.

A Different Genre of COMA

A final word about the passage I've selected. I'm moving from an Old Testament narrative (1 Kings 16) to a New Testament Gospel (John 5). As I've taught people how to study the Bible *a la* COMA over the years, I've noticed that many of them do better with some kinds of literature than with others. For example, they may love Old Testament stories and find it easy to spot life lessons in such—but have a hard time getting into the densely worded theological arguments of Paul's epistles. Others, however, can't get enough of Romans or Colossians—but they really struggle to squeeze something for their lives out of the prophets Amos or Obadiah. (OK, who *doesn't* struggle to squeeze something out of Amos or Obadiah?)

So I am giving you a taste of two different biblical genres in this chapter. You may gravitate more to one than the other, but I hope you'll get a feel for how COMA works with both. In fact, in the appendix you will find the results of a COMA study of three additional kinds of biblical literature: Old Testament poetry (Ecclesiastes 2), Old Testament prophecy (Isaiah 14), and New Testament epistle (Hebrews 2). The Study Guide at the end of this chapter will ask you to do your own COMA studies of these passages. After you've completed your work, you can compare it with what I've provided in the appendix.

As you're working on the Study Guide passages, you may want to pull out (or purchase) your copy of *Context* and turn to the chapter on *literary settings*. Each kind of biblical literature comes with its own rules of interpretation. These rules are covered quite simply in *Context* and may shed some light on the passages you'll be studying. Are you ready to COMA John 5?

A COMA for John 5

Context. The author of this Gospel is John, who repeatedly identifies himself as "the disciple whom Jesus loved" (13:23; 19:26; 20:2; 21:7, 20, 24). Don't think of this as one-upmanship on John's part (like the child who boasts, "Mom loves me best"). He's not comparing himself with the other disciples; he's just noting the closeness of his own relationship with Jesus. That makes this Gospel a very intimate, firsthand account. It is written by someone who saw what Jesus did and heard what Jesus taught. John wrote down these eyewitness observations some time before the end of the first century. His Gospel has a different feel than the Gospels of Matthew, Mark, and Luke and includes things that the others leave out.

John tells us the purpose for his book in 20:30–31: "Jesus did many other miraculous signs in the presence of his disciples, which are not recorded in this book. But these are written that you may believe that Jesus is the Christ, the Son of God, and that by believing you may have life in his name." John wants to lead people to faith in Christ. To that end, he describes some of Jesus' miracles, which point to His true identity and saving power.

John calls these miracles "signs." There are seven of them described in this Gospel. And the healing of the lame man, at the beginning of chapter 5, is one of them. This event took place during "a feast of the Jews" (v. 1), which probably refers to one of three annual celebrations that brought thousands of religious pilgrims to Jerusalem. The location of the healing was a pool called Bethesda that had a reputation for curative powers.

Observations-Meanings-Applications. This is a long chapter (forty-seven verses) and it contains many, many details that might be cited as observations. A person could spend an entire week in John 5. But if you're following the four-year Bible reading schedule (available at *biblesavvy.com*), you must cover it in a single day. Is this too fast a pace?

Well, first let me point out that this is why I don't care for the read-through-the-Bible-in-a-year schedule. If you were on that plan, you'd not only be reading John 5 in a day but would also be reading a couple of Old Testament chapters and a psalm or two on the same day! At the other extreme, if you insist on taking several days to read and study, say, John 5 because of its rich content, it will be years before you make it through the entire Bible. So one chapter of reading per day is about the right pace (i.e., the four-year Bible reading schedule)—even though passages like John 5 will be a challenge to cover in the time allotted.

Remember that your goal is not to observe every possible detail of the text. Make a handful of observations and choose one of them to develop into a message and application. Here is a sampling of what I saw in John 5.

Observation: Jesus repeatedly referred to Himself as one who had been *sent* by the Father (vv. 23–24, 30, 36–38). This verb reminds us that He came to earth for a special purpose. Jesus was on a mission from God.

Message: Jesus lived with a keen consciousness that He had been *sent* to save the world.

Application: Elsewhere Jesus says that He sends His followers into the world in the same way that the Father had sent Him. Am I keeping my *sent*-ness in the forefront of my thinking? My life purpose must be to bring the good news of salvation to others. Pray for opportunities to talk about Christ today.

Observation: Jesus was very careful to do only what the Father wanted Him to do (a *repeated idea* in vv. 19, 30, 36). He had a very focused agenda.

Message: The temptation to do too much, to pack a schedule too full, will wear a person out! Let God set the agenda.

Application: Look over the day's "To Do" list. Is there anything on it that is a *good* idea but not a *God* idea? Only engage in tasks to which God is calling me. Don't add another activity to my schedule without asking: *Lord, is this something You want me to do?*

Observation: The following all bore testimony to Jesus (circle the numerous occurrences of *testify/testimony*): John the Baptist (v. 33); Jesus' works (v. 36); God the Father (v. 37); Scriptures (v. 39); and Moses (v. 46). There is plenty of evidence to substantiate that Jesus is who He claims to be.

Message: Be confident and bold in asserting Jesus' claims for Himself!

Application: This observation brings to my mind the books of apologist Lee Strobel. I will pick up an extra copy of *The Case for Christ* or *The Case for Faith* and pass it on to an unbelieving friend.

Observation: My curiosity is piqued (*something striking*) by the question Jesus asks the lame man: "Do you want to get well?" (v. 6). Isn't the answer to this inquiry a no-brainer? Of course; why would a lame man *not* want to get well? My footnote suggests a couple of reasons why Jesus asked the question. First, the man might have found begging to be a profitable profession. And second, he might have given up on ever being healed.

Message: Sometimes we don't really want or expect God to intervene in our lives.

Application: Is there something I'm not praying about (or have stopped praying about) because I've concluded that God is just not going to do anything about it? Where have I accepted the status quo—instead of challenging it in prayer?

Observation: Something else grabs my attention: after Jesus healed this guy He told him to stop sinning or something worse would happen (v. 14)! I know that sickness is not necessarily the result of sin in a person's life (see John 9:1–3). But evidently, on occasion, it *is*.

Message: God sometimes uses illness or hardship to get our attention about sin in our lives.

Application: Ask God if there is something behind my health problems. Any sin to be acknowledged and uprooted?

Observation: The religious rulers were such weenies! (Sorry, it was the first derogatory name that came to mind.) In verses 9–10 they accost the healed man for carrying his mat on the Sabbath—something which they claim is against Moses' law. It really isn't a transgression of the law. It just violates their interpretation of how the Sabbath law should be lived out.

Message: Beware of man-made rules—and don't let them become a yardstick by which others are measured.

Application: I must be especially careful that spiritual disciplines (e.g., Bible reading, tithing, serving the poor) don't become legalistic rules by which I attempt to earn God's favor.

I've just listed six observations from John 5 that led to messages and applications for my life. And yet I haven't scratched the surface of this chapter of John's Gospel. Without taking the time to develop the following thoughts, let me point out several other observations I made while reading the passage. In the category of *something striking*, I was struck by how much the religious leaders were diligent Bible students—yet blind to what the Bible taught about Christ (vv. 39, 40). I was also unsettled by Jesus' accusation that His antagonists preferred the praise of one another to the praise that comes from God (v. 44; ouch! that hits close to home).

And here are a few *truths about God the Son* (i.e., Jesus) I noted: He sovereignly chose to heal the lame man, in spite of there being no mention of faith on the guy's part (vv. 8–9); He called God by the intimate name of *Father*—something that Jews avoided doing, and which was interpreted as a claim to being equal with God (vv. 17–18); He referred to Himself as the source of life (vv. 21, 26); and He warned that mankind would face Him as judge (vv. 22, 27).

Wow! Any one of these observations is worth running with. Significant messages could be drawn from them and life-transforming applications made of those messages. What did you come up with?

Now it's time to try your hand at using COMA with a few more passages of different genres. Turn to the Study Guide and go for it. And when you're finished, don't forget to compare your results with the COMA insights from these Bible chapters that are provided in the appendix.

Study Guide

Icebreaker

What kinds of things are you most observant about (i.e., you notice details)? In what areas of life do you wish you were more observant?

1. Do a COMA study of Ecclesiastes 2. (Compare your results with the appendix.)

   Context:

   Observations (theme; repeating words or ideas; something striking; truths about God):

   Message (from one of your observations):

   Application:

2. 😊😊😊 Do a COMA study of Isaiah 14. (Compare your results with the appendix.)

Context:

Observations (theme; repeating words or ideas; something striking; truths about God):

Message (from one of your observations):

Application:

3. 😊😊😊 Do a COMA study of Hebrews 2. (Compare your results with the appendix.)

Context:

Observations (theme; repeating words or ideas; something striking; truths about God):

Message (from one of your observations):

Application:

4. 🗣 Do a COMA study of Leviticus 4, or Psalm 139, or 1 John 4. (Your pick. How big a challenge do you want? You won't find any help in the appendix. It's just you . . . and the Holy Spirit.)

Context:

Observations (theme; repeating words or ideas; something striking; truths about God):

Message (from one of your observations):

Application:

A Daily Discipline

I WAS FLIPPING THROUGH the TV channels after watching the news one night, and I came across a lady preacher. Her name was Pastor Bambi. No offense to any reader of this book named Bambi, but if I were a lady preacher with that name, who was trying to draw a television audience, I think I would change my name to something that has more gravitas. Maybe something with a biblical ring to it—like Pastor Esther or Pastor Rachel.

There was something else about her program that caught my attention. Pastor Bambi was offering her viewers miracles. Splashed across my TV screen in big bold letters were the words: *Miracle Healings!!* Well, I believe that God sometimes miraculously heals people today. So I had no problem with that. But the next set of big bold letters read: *Miracle Debt Cancellations!!* Really? Miracle debt cancellations? No doubt a lot of people who flip through TV channels late at night are struggling with debt. That's a big problem in our country today. But how should we be addressing the problem?

Should you and I be hoping for "miracle debt cancellations"? Should we watch Pastor Bambi's TV program, pray with her at the end of the show for our debt to be removed, and then expect to hear the next day from Visa Card, or our home mortgage company, or the government's student loan department: "Good news! You don't owe us anything! Somebody paid your bill!"?

Well, I'll tell you how we fix people's debt problems at our church. We encourage men and women to sign up for a nine-week Financial Peace University small group. FPU is a very practical study that's been put together by financial expert Dave Ramsey.[1] It trains people—in a small-group setting with other eager participants—how to make money, save money, budget money, and give money. This requires a lot of hard work and discipline! But we've seen scores of people climb out of debt and begin to enjoy life. These people weren't waiting around for some miracle debt cancellation.

Don't get me wrong. We believe in miracles at our church. And God does do *financial* miracles in our lives from time to time. But God also seems to expect from us a certain amount of hard work and discipline—in whatever area of our lives we hope to grow in. This is even true of our spiritual development. Look at what the Bible says about this: "Train yourself to be godly. For physical training is of some value, but godliness has value for all things" (1 Timothy 4:7b–8a).

The first sentence is straightforward: "Train yourself to be godly." The word *train* in these verses is the Greek verb *gymnazo*. Now, you don't have to be a Bible scholar to deduce that *gymnazo* is the word from which we get *gymnasium*—the place where we go to exercise and work out. That's what's required for godliness, Paul says. That's what's necessary for spiritual growth: exercising and working out.

The apostle Paul even likens *godliness* training to *physical* training in these verses. The same sort of discipline is required for both endeavors. In other words, spiritual growth isn't something that just happens to us. It's something we've got to work at. This is especially true when it comes to the practice of applying the Bible to our lives. Bible application takes work. It takes *daily discipline*. In this chapter you'll discover four factors that will help you develop that discipline.

The Role of the Holy Spirit

My brother-in-law recently told me a story about his five-year-old grandson. Little Cole is a preschooler. And he's a bit on the hyperactive side, which means he's always getting in trouble at the Christian school he attends. When Cole's mommy arrives to pick him up each day, he's frequently seated in the principal's office.

That's where she found him a couple of weeks ago. His mom looked at him sternly and asked, "What's the problem, Cole?" Now, Cole has a hard time saying his *v*'s—they come out as *b*'s. So, he looked forlornly at his mommy and replied,

"I can't get da debil out of my heart."

Cole isn't the only one who's got a problem with the debil in his heart. We all do! And no amount of effort on our part is going to remove the debil from our hearts. This is something that only God can do. Only God can liberate us from Satan's death-grip and make us spiritually alive.

In John 3, we read the story of a religious leader by the name of Nicodemus (I like that name), who visited Jesus one night. Nicodemus approached Jesus under the cloak of darkness because he didn't want anyone to see him soliciting spiritual input. After all, Nicodemus was supposed to be a guy with spiritual *answers*, not spiritual *questions*.

Jesus cut right to the chase with Nicodemus. He told Nick that if he wanted spiritual life, he'd have to be born again. And then Jesus explained that being born again isn't something you can do to yourself. It's something that only God's *Spirit* can do to people. But God's Spirit won't do this to you (we learn elsewhere in Scripture) until you surrender your life to Jesus Christ. Only when you sincerely ask Jesus to forgive your sin and lead your life, will the Holy Spirit come to live on the inside and make you spiritually alive.

Just as the Holy Spirit is the force behind your spiritual *birth*, He is also the power behind your spiritual *growth*. Remember those verses we looked at in 1 Timothy 4 a few moments ago? They said that "training to be godly" requires hard work. Spiritual growth won't just *happen* to you—you'll have to go after it. But where do the desire and the discipline to "go after it" come from? From the Holy Spirit.

> **YOU'LL HAVE to go after it [spiritual growth]. But the desire and the discipline to "go after it" come from the Holy Spirit.**

Let me give you an analogy: growing spiritually is like sailing a boat. Can you picture yourself doing that? Sue and I lived on Cape Cod years ago, and we occasionally went sailing with friends. So, it's not too hard for me to picture the scene I'm about to describe to you. Your sails are hoisted, you've got a sunshiny day, you've got miles of open water in front of you, and you've got the basic skills of sailing under your belt. What's the only thing you lack? A good breeze!! Have you ever been on a sailboat when there was no wind? You didn't go anywhere. Boooooring.

The Holy Spirit is the wind in the sails of your spiritual growth. (Jesus used wind as a word picture to talk about the Holy Spirit with Nicodemus in John 3—maybe because *wind* and *spirit* come from the same Hebrew word, *ruach*.) The daily discipline you need to apply God's Word to your life—to pick up a Bible, read it, and put it into practice—must come from the Holy Spirit. If you try to do this by sheer personal willpower, you'll give it up in no time. It'll be about as enjoyable as sailing on a day with no wind.

Here are a couple of verses from Galatians 3 that back up this point that I'm making: "I would like to learn just one thing from you: Did you receive the Spirit by observing the law, or by believing what you heard? Are you so foolish? After beginning with the Spirit, are you now trying to attain your goal by human effort?" (Galatians 3:2–3).

Do you follow Paul's argument here? He asks the Galatians how the Holy Spirit came into their lives in the first place. Was it the result of observing the law, Paul asks. In other words, was it the result of their personal effort? Was it the result of keeping God's rules? Was it the result of pulling themselves up by their spiritual bootstraps? No! The Galatians initially received the Holy Spirit by simply believing—by simply surrendering their lives to Jesus Christ, as I've already explained. That's how the Holy Spirit comes to live in people.

OK, Paul continues, if that's how you Galatians experienced spiritual *birth*, how do you think you experience spiritual *growth*? Is it now all up to you? Does the discipline that's required for training in godliness come from within you? Are you supposed to just suck it up and get 'er done? Is it a case of "three yards and a grass stain"? No! You need to depend on the Holy Spirit for both the desire and the discipline to grow spiritually.

If the reading, journaling, and applying of the Bible is not yet a part of your daily routine—or if it comes and goes—you need to ask the Holy Spirit to put wind in your sails. You will never consistently walk the Word until the Holy Spirit motivates and empowers you to do so. Make this a matter of prayer. (But keep in mind that you won't even be able to pray earnestly for this discipline unless the Holy Spirit enables you to pray earnestly. Start your asking there.)

The Role of Personal Effort

OK. I may be confusing you. My first point has been that spiritual growth must come from the Holy Spirit, *not* from personal effort. Now, my second point is that spiritual growth comes from personal effort. Huh?

Let me illustrate this second factor with an anecdote, an unusual story that appeared in a news magazine (so it must be true). The owner of a new recreational vehicle had a traffic accident after making a rather poor choice. According to the news report, the guy put his RV on the interstate for the first time, got it up to speed, and then pushed the cruise control button. At this point, with his RV in an automatic mode, and with nothing in front of him but open road, this guy decided to get up from his seat and make a sandwich for himself in the kitchenette.

Too late, he realized that driving his RV required some involvement on his part. Big mistake!

I know some Christ followers who make a similar blunder with regard to their spiritual journey. They assume that since the Holy Spirit now indwells them, they are on some sort of spiritual "autopilot." There is no need for them to do anything. They don't believe that training in godliness should involve rigorous exercise. It's simply a matter of waiting for the Holy Spirit to overwhelm them with the urge and the power to do the right thing.

Years ago, one of the elders in the church that I pastored out East lived by this approach. As a self-employed commercial artist, he could schedule his day any way he pleased. Well, some days, he would get the urge to study his Bible—so he would. All day! But other days he wouldn't feel inclined to pick up God's Word—so he wouldn't. In fact, he would occasionally go a couple of weeks without reading his Bible at all (not good for a church elder).

The guy drove me nuts. But he was convinced that he should never ever do anything of a spiritual nature unless he felt an overwhelming leading of the Holy Spirit to do so. He believed that if something required effort on his part, it must be wrong. Not surprisingly, his spiritual life was a mess! Totally erratic. Huge ups and downs. The apostle Peter has something to say to those who are tempted to take this approach, who assume that spiritual growth should be an effortless endeavor:

For this very reason, *make every effort* to add to your faith goodness; and to goodness, knowledge; and to knowledge, self-control; and to self-control, perseverance; and to perseverance, godliness; and to godliness, brotherly kindness; and to brotherly kindness, love. For if you possess these qualities in increasing measure, they will keep you from being ineffective and unproductive in your knowledge of our Lord Jesus Christ. (2 Peter 1:5–8, emphasis added)

The theme of the above Bible passage is spiritual growth. Peter identifies eight qualities that ought to characterize the life of a Christ follower "in increasing measure." Please note that one of these qualities is *knowledge.* In fact, Peter mentions knowledge twice in this passage, at the beginning and at the end (v. 5 and v. 8). He exhorts us to grow in our knowledge of Jesus Christ. How do we acquire such knowledge? Doesn't this require getting into the Bible? Absolutely.

And what does Peter say about the way in which we should go about a pursuit of Bible knowledge? Look at the second phrase in verse 5: "make every effort." So spiritual growth requires knowledge of Jesus Christ; knowledge of Jesus Christ requires getting into the Bible; and getting into the Bible requires *personal effort.*

Personal effort is not inconsistent with relying on the Holy Spirit to put the wind in your sails. Personal effort and the Holy Spirit go hand in hand. Of course, if you try to grow spiritually on nothing but personal effort, you're going to feel like you're pushing a rock up a hill with your nose. You need the Holy Spirit's empowerment. But on the other hand, if you try to grow spiritually by always waiting for the Holy Spirit to move you to do the right thing, your growth is going to be erratic, inconsistent, whimsical. You need to *make every effort*—as Peter says.

PERSONAL EFFORT and the Holy Spirit go hand in hand.

Let me give you a picture of how the Holy Spirit and personal effort work hand in hand. It's a picture that God paints for us in the Old Testament. After God delivered His people from slavery in Egypt, He led them to the very edge of Canaan. And then God made them a promise. God promised them victory. God promised to drive out their enemies. God promised to give them the land (which is why it was known as the Promised Land). But right alongside these sorts of promises, God repeatedly challenged His people to be courageous and fight hard!

So, which was it? Was God going to drive out their enemies and give them the land, or were they supposed to fight for it? The correct answer is: YES! Acquiring the Promised Land was a both/and kind of thing. And that's the same way we're to pursue spiritual growth today—by *both* relying on

God's Spirit *and* making every personal effort.

I frequently talk with Christ followers who wonder if something is wrong in their pursuit of spiritual growth, because it feels like such an effort at times. Why don't they leap out of bed in the morning and grab their Bible, eager to meet with God? What's wrong with them? Should they just stay in bed until the Holy Spirit gives them the urge to get up and read God's Word?

Let me answer that question with a story from the life of Harry Ironside. Dr. Ironside was a great Bible teacher in the middle of the twentieth century. On one occasion, he was speaking on the campus of a Christian college, and a student asked him a personal question after his lecture: "How do you manage to get up every morning and study the Bible?" Here was Dr. Ironside's response. (You may have to read this next sentence twice, since it's so profound.) He said: "I just get up."

Deep stuff, eh? If you determine to read your Bible every morning (or at some other set time during the day), there will be many days when you don't feel like doing it. But don't wait for the Holy Spirit to move you. Just get up! The same advice applies to your participation in a small group, where you study and apply the Bible with friends. Personal confession: There are many times that I don't feel like going to my early Wednesday morning men's group when my alarm goes off. (OK, I admit it. And I'm a pastor. But let me finish.) However,

I am always glad to be at my men's group once I'm there. And I'm super pumped by the time I'm driving away from it.

The daily discipline of applying God's Word to your life requires the empowerment of the Holy Spirit, the exertion of personal effort, and . . .

The Role of Godly Habits

Have you ever tried to break a bad habit? Have you ever tried to stop smoking, biting your nails, watching too much TV, texting while driving, or leaving the toilet seat up? It's hard to break a bad habit, isn't it? Habits seem to have a power of their own. Which is why it's so helpful to develop *godly habits*. Godly habits have the power to propel you on to spiritual growth. Whether it's the habit of gathering for worship with other believers *every* week, or the habit of giving God the first 10 percent of *every* paycheck, or the habit of reading your Bible *every* day—godly habits will grow you up in Christ.

Unfortunately, far too many Christ followers fail to develop godly habits. Sometimes it's because they're lazy. Sometimes it's because they get bored with routine. Sometimes it's because they object that godly habits (churchgoing, tithing, Bible reading, etc.) are legalistic—nothing but rules, rules, rules.

I get so tired of hearing that last argument. Why don't

we call it *legalistic* when someone runs ten miles every day in preparation for a marathon? Why don't we call it *legalistic* when someone does homework every day in order to graduate? Why don't we call it *legalistic* when someone brushes their teeth every day so as to avoid cavities? Why is it only *legalistic* when someone practices godly habits out of a desire to grow spiritually?

Let me suggest to you that anyone who ever excels at anything—be it piano, golf, sales, parenthood, gardening—gets there by practicing certain habits. They don't just "wing it." Keep that in mind as you read the following verse: "Do your best to present yourself to God as one approved, a workman who does not need to be ashamed and who correctly handles the word of truth" (2 Timothy 2:15).

What does God want you to excel at? Handling His Word! He wants you to be able to handle the Bible like a skilled workman handles his tools. Now, I'm pretty sure that skilled workmen don't become skilled until they've put hours and hours of practice into using those tools. They become skilled out of *habit*.

WHAT DOES God want you to excel at? Handling His Word!

And so I want to challenge you to become habitual in your handling of God's Word. Let me give you some key ingredients that would contribute to the development of this godly habit—three pairs of ingredients. (By the way, if these look familiar, it's because I touched on the same ingredients in *Foundation*, the second book in the Bible Savvy series. But I'm not averse to repeating myself in order to drive home an important point.)

A time and a place. Many people find early morning to be the best time of day for getting into the Bible. One advantage of this time slot is that there is typically nothing else competing for your attention—except sleep. Those who try to read their Bibles later in the day often find themselves distracted by other concerns. Or something comes up unexpectedly that bumps their Bible reading. So meeting with God first thing in the morning is often the best plan. However, if a long lunch break or a quiet moment after you get the kids to bed works best for you, go for it. Just remember that there's a better chance of the Bible becoming a habit if you read it *at the same time* every day.

Same with the location. Find a place that works for you and stick to it. It may be in your pickup truck as you sit in the parking lot at work. It may be at a local coffee shop, assuming that you can screen out the white noise. It may be at your kitchen table. It may be on the treadmill—as long as you make time for writing something down after you're done walking or running. What time and place would work best for you? Lock them in, right now. Start tomorrow.

A Bible and a reading schedule. You don't want just any kind of Bible, right? You want . . . (If you're not saying the right answer out loud at this point, all my nagging has been ineffective.) You want a *study* Bible. Make it an *NIV Study Bible*—or a similar study Bible—with all the helpful book introductions, explanatory footnotes, cross-references, a concordance, and maps.

Let's say you're Bible-ready. Where are you going to start reading? Let me give you several suggestions, schedule-wise. Pick whichever one suits you best. If you're brand new to the Bible, you might want to start in a Gospel—one of the four biographies of Jesus. I think Mark is the easiest place to begin. It's sixteen chapters long, so if you read one per day, you'll finish the book in two to three weeks. Way to go!

IF YOU'RE brand new to the Bible, you might want to start reading in a Gospel.

For most people, I'd recommend the four-year Bible reading schedule that you can find on the *biblesavvy.com* website. You'll go through the Old Testament once and the New Testament twice during that time period. It's a very doable pace—one or two chapters a day, five days a week. The brisk pace of a one-year schedule will frequently leave you falling behind and feeling guilty.

Speaking of avoiding guilt, you can also read through

the Bible without using any schedule at all. You'll never feel pushed or prodded. Simply pick a book of the Bible to begin with, read one chapter a day, put your bookmark between the pages, and the next time you read just pick up where you left off. (If you miss a day or two, you miss a day or two. No pressure to catch up with a predetermined schedule.) When you get done with that book of the Bible, go to the table of contents and check it off. Then start with a new book.

Here's one last reading schedule approach. If you're in a small group and you're using a curriculum that's taking you through a book of the Bible, spread your homework out over the course of a week (i.e., that's your reading schedule). Don't do it all the night before your group meets. It's just like eating. Much better to ingest some food every day than to stuff yourself once a week at an all-you-can-eat buffet.

A notebook and COMA. I would encourage you to go back and review chapter 2, "From Text to Life." Have you begun using COMA in your daily Bible reading? The *context-observations-message-application* approach will ensure that you *walk* the Word. Following the four steps of this acronym may feel as awkward as learning to ride a bike at first. But they say (don't ask me who *they* are) that it takes thirty days to develop any good habit. So, try giving COMA a one-month trial, writing something down each day, and see what it does for your spiritual growth.

Role Models

This fourth factor is icing on the cake. Having role models can strengthen your daily discipline of applying God's Word to your life (alongside of *the Holy Spirit, your personal effort,* and *godly habits*). Positive role models have a way of inspiring us to do the right thing. This is probably why the apostle Paul frequently urged the readers of his epistles to imitate him (see his requests in Philippians 3:17; 4:9; 1 Corinthians 4:16; 11:1; 1 Thessalonians 1:6; 2 Thessalonians 3:7, 9; and 2 Timothy 3:10, 14).

These role models don't even have to be well-known Christ followers if they exemplify good habits. I just finished reading a biography about Ron Santo. Ron was the all-star third baseman of the Chicago Cubs who recently joined baseball's Hall of Fame. He was a boyhood hero of mine. All the infielders on my Little League team tried to imitate Ron's hustle—diving for ground balls, even when they were hit right to us. After Ron's playing days concluded, he became a radio announcer for the Cubs. It was a job that he held right up until he passed away.

Ron had severe diabetes. He had to have one leg amputated . . . and then the other. And his diabetes was complicated by heart trouble and cancer. But as I read Ron's biography, I was so impressed by his upbeat, "can do" spirit. Getting around on two prosthetic legs didn't slow him down.

He bounded up and down the stairways to the announcer's booth at Wrigley Field. He even played a lot of golf and could hit a pretty long tee shot. As I was reading this stuff, I felt convicted about all the times that I complain about my aches and pains. All the times that I complain about having to work out to stay in shape. I decided that Ron Santo is a good role model for me when it comes to pushing myself physically.

WHEN IT COMES to pushing yourself *spiritually*, do you have any good role models?

Do you have any good role models, when it comes to pushing yourself *spiritually*? Do you complain—at least to yourself—that reading and applying the Bible is just too much work? Is that why you've neglected to make it a daily discipline? I want you to consider, as a role model, a guy whose story is told in Robert Sumner's book *The Wonder of the Word of God*.[2]

This is a true story, although Sumner doesn't tell us the guy's name. He lived in Kansas City, and was severely injured in an explosion at work. The man's face was badly disfigured. He lost his eyesight, as well as the use of both hands. Having recently become a Christ follower, his greatest disappointment was that he could no longer read his Bible. But then he heard about a lady in England who'd learned to read Braille with her lips. Unfortunately, the nerve endings in his own lips had been destroyed by the explosion. One day, however, he touched some raised Braille letters with his tongue and found that he could distinguish the characters.

At last count, he'd read through the Bible four times—with his tongue! Now, there's an inspirational role model for you. Do you still think that the daily discipline of reading and applying God's Word is beyond you?

I could tell you many more stories that are far less dramatic. I could tell you about my eighty-something-year-old mom and dad who still read and apply the Bible every day of their lives. I could tell you about a guy who attends my church and informed me that he'd grown up with a reading disorder. Books had never been his friends. But he was determined to befriend *God's* Book. So he picked up a Bible and started working through just one paragraph at a time. Today, he's not only a Bible reader—he's discovered that this daily discipline has given him the skill to read other printed materials as well.

I could tell you about the high school girls that I saw in a coffee shop the other day. They were huddled over their Bibles, and I thought I recognized a couple of them from my church. One girl approached me after their gathering broke up, and explained that since our youth ministry's House Groups were taking a break for the summer, she and her friends were getting together on their own to study the Bible.

I could tell you about some of the guys in my Wednesday morning men's group who are brand new to the Bible—but now they're reading it and coming up with great applications for their lives. As a matter of fact, I'm always personally challenged by the applications they come up with. And it bugs me when I hear people who've been Christ followers for years say that they prefer being in a group of "mature" believers with whom they can do "deep" Bible study. What makes a Bible study deep? Learning the Hebrew meaning of some Old Testament word? Tracing the route of Paul's third missionary journey on a first-century world map? Give me a break! I think "deep" Bible study happens when people put God's Word into practice. That's why some of *my* role models in this regard are beginners.

There are role models all around you—people who are digging into God's Word and applying it to their lives as a daily discipline. What about you? Today would be a good day to start.

Study Guide

Icebreaker

In what areas of your life are you disciplined? In what areas of your life do you wish you were more disciplined? Why are you more disciplined in some areas than in others?

1. Read 1 Timothy 4:7b, 8. In what ways might training in godliness be like physical training?

   Why does Paul say that training in godliness trumps physical training? What might be included on the list of "all things" for which godliness has value?

2. What four factors contribute to your spiritual growth? Briefly describe why each one is important.

3. Explain why the Holy Spirit's empowerment and personal effort must be balanced as you pursue spiritual growth (i.e., what happens when either of these is neglected).

What Old Testament picture portrays this balance?

4. What do you think is the difference between godly habits and legalistic practices? How might you keep the former from morphing into the latter in your life?

5. What would be the best time and place for you to daily spend time with God in His Word? Why?

6. Which Bible reading schedule (i.e., of the several recommended in this chapter) would work best for you? Why?

7. Do a COMA study of 2 Corinthians 4.

   Context:

   Observations (3–4):

   Message (and title):

   Application:

8. Why do you think Paul urged others to imitate him?

What do you learn about the example Paul set from the following verses: Philippians 3:17; 4:9; 1 Corinthians 4:15–17; 1 Thessalonians 1:4–6; 2 Thessalonians 3:6–10; 2 Timothy 3:10–11?

9. Who models spiritual growth for you? What can you learn from this person's example?

Why are spiritual role models important?

Appendix:
Additional COMA
Passages

IN THE STUDY GUIDE FOR CHAPTER 3
you did your own COMA study of Ecclesiastes 2, Isaiah 14, and Hebrews 2. As a sample of how it may look, here are my own COMA studies of these passages. (If you haven't completed all three passages at the end of chapter 3, no peeking at these; first finish and then come back.)

Ecclesiastes 2

Context. Although the writer of Ecclesiastes is never identified by name, there are many signs in the book that point to Solomon as its author. He is referred to as: a "son of David" (1:1); a "king over Israel" (1:12); a builder of "great projects" (2:4); a guy who "amassed silver and gold" (2:8); a man who found some women to be "a snare" (7:26); and a teacher of many proverbs (12:9). Sure sounds like Solomon to me—or someone who is putting himself in Solomon's sandals as a writing device.

Solomon reigned over Israel during its golden era (around

900 BC, give or take a few decades). But even though he'd had it all and seen it all, Solomon was pretty cynical about what life had to offer. Ecclesiastes is the reflections of an old man who learned the hard way that only God can give a person lasting satisfaction. Because this is a book of poetry, expect Solomon to use picturesque language to get his point across.

Observations-Messages-Applications. Ecclesiastes 2 is a gold mine of *repeating words or ideas.* Often when I am reading through a chapter of the Bible and come across a repeating word, I will circle that word each time it pops up. But if I come across a second repeating word, I will put a box around every occurrence of it—so as to distinguish it from the circled word. If a third repeating word shows up, it gets bracketed. And so it goes. Well, in Ecclesiastes 2, there are so many repeating words or ideas that I ran out of devices by which to identify them.

Here are six observations from Ecclesiastes 2, each with an accompanying message and application:

> *Observation.* Solomon was a huge pursuer of *pleasure* (a word that's found in verses 1, 2, 10; its synonym, *delight*, is also used)—but it never brought him fulfillment.
>
> *Message.* Pleasure, in and of itself, is empty.

Application. I tend to overuse the renting of a good movie as an escape. The pleasure of such is short-lived. The next time I'm inclined to pick up something at Redbox, I will look instead for a way to connect with God.

Observation. Solomon tried to find meaning in his work—to no avail (see *work/toil/labor* in verses 17, 18, 19, 20, 21, 22, 23, 24—more than twenty-five times in Ecclesiastes overall).

Message. Lasting satisfaction can't be found in a job.

Application. I work too many hours—a habit that to some extent is fueled by the accolades I receive from others and the importance of my vocation. But I must start saying "no" to long hours. I must honor my day off.

Observation. Solomon discovered a wide variety of life-pursuits to be "meaningless" (a word that describes a passing breath and which is used eight times in this chapter and thirty-five times in Ecclesiastes as a whole). Solomon also refers to these life-pursuits as a "chasing after the wind" (three times in this chapter and nine times in the book). It must be noted, however, that the reason these activities prove to be empty is because they are most often pursued as an end in themselves and for benefits in *this* world. Solomon unmasks our all-too-often *present*-world perspective with the repeating phrase "under the sun" (six times in this chapter and twenty-nine times in the book).

Message. Nothing in this world can produce a lasting, joyous sense of significance.

Application. Make a list of five things (or activities) from which I try to gain significance or happiness (family members not included). Acknowledge to God the futility of this pursuit.

Observation. I am struck by the fact (aha! *something striking*) that even *wisdom* (which pops up ten times in Ecclesiastes 2) is derided by Solomon as meaningless (v. 15). Wisdom is meaningless? Only in the sense that, apart from God, it doesn't change a person's ultimate fate.

Message. Wisdom and knowledge shouldn't be pursued as an end in themselves.

Application. I am an insatiable learner, always reading. I need to return to my practice of evaluating and summarizing in an electronic file what I've just finished reading—from the standpoint of what that reading contributes to eternal values and objectives.

Observation. Solomon reached the point of actually *hating* his life and the things he'd worked for (2:17, 18). His honest despair and strong language jumped off the page at me.

Message. When life is in the pits, that's often an indication that the wrong sources have been trusted to provide fulfillment.

Application. The next time I'm discouraged (I probably won't have long to wait), I will ask myself the question: *What am I currently depending on to make me happy?*

Observation. Here's an eye-opening *truth about God* from 2:24–26: Only He can enable us to enjoy anything in this life (i.e., in a thorough and lasting way). The footnote in my *NIV Study Bible* says that these verses are *the heart of Ecclesiastes,* introducing a theme that's repeated in: 3:12, 13, 22; 5:18–20; 8:15; 9:7; and 12:13.

Message. The search for significance must begin and end with God.

Application. Don't let my daily "quiet times" (a.k.a. devotions, appointments with God, personal Bible study, etc.) become mechanical. Evaluate whether I'm just going through the motions or genuinely connecting with God. Am I taking time to worship—since worship rekindles my heart's desire for God?

Isaiah 14

Context. Isaiah was written by a prophet whose name literally meant "the Lord saves"—a fitting name, since he had much to say about God's coming salvation. Isaiah saw the northern kingdom of Israel fall to the Assyrians in 722 BC, and he warned the southern kingdom of Judah that a similar fate awaited them if they didn't repent of their sin and turn back to God. Isaiah spent most of his life in Jerusalem, the capital city of Judah. The prophets Amos, Hosea, and Micah were his contemporaries. Tradition says that Isaiah met his death at the hands of wicked king Manasseh—who sawed him in two!

Isaiah 14 begins with a promise of restoration. Isaiah describes a time in the future when God would bring His people back from foreign captivity and resettle them in their own land. Bible scholars assert that there are three possible interpretations of this resettlement. It could be a description of Judah's return from Babylonian exile a couple hundred years in the future. Or, it could be a figurative description of people being gathered into the church through faith in Christ (who is called God's *Servant* in Isaiah) over the last two thousand years. Or, finally, it could describe the millennial kingdom that Christ will inaugurate when He returns to rule over this earth.

Did I learn all this stuff in seminary? Nope, I picked it up from reading the introduction and various footnotes to Isaiah in my *NIV Study Bible*. That's also where I learned that the *theme* of Isaiah 14 is *a prophecy against Babylon*—a diatribe that began back in chapter 13. What's amazing about such a prophecy is that Babylon was not yet a superpower when Isaiah wrote that it would one day conquer and exile Judah. And what's more, Isaiah prophesied that Babylon, after conquering other nations, would itself be conquered.

> *Observations-Messages-Applications.* Here are five observations about Isaiah 14, followed by corresponding messages and applications.

> *Observation.* Isaiah's prophecy against Babylon, the *theme* of chapter 14 (see the heading in chapter 13), begins a ten-chapter section that describes the coming destruction of one wicked nation after another. God's people were probably cheering when they got this news—but their euphoria was cut short when they arrived at Isaiah 22. Because God had plans to punish wicked Jerusalem as well.

Message. God punishes wickedness wherever it is found —even in His own people.

Application. Make a list of three or four sins that especially aggravate me when I see them in others. Now, look for signs of those same sins in my own life and repent of them.

Observation. The first-person pronoun "I" is repeated, again and again, in verses 13–14. These "I" statements are the arrogant boasting of Babylon—putting itself on par with God!

Message. Bragging is audacious. It takes credit for things that God has done.

Application. Be careful of self-promotion in conversation with others. Do I leave people impressed with me or with God?

Observation. I am struck by what will be the ultimate fate of proud Babylon. The description in verse 11 is one that any middle schooler would love: "Maggots are spread out beneath you and worms cover you." Gross!

Message. The horrific demise of Babylon underscores the fact that God hates pride and will not put up with it for long. (As 1 Peter 5:5 says, "God opposes the proud but gives grace to the humble.")

Application. This heightens the sense of my previous application. Bragging is not only foolish and audacious; it is also dangerous—because it puts me in the same camp as God's enemies. (Did you catch the footnote that points out that this passage has been considered to be a description of Satan's fall? Pride is the identifying mark of God's archenemy!) Be on the lookout for evidences of pride in my life and deal with it severely.

Observation. Throughout this chapter God is described as the one who will deliver His people from bondage and destroy their enemies (a wonderful *truth about God*). But I am especially impressed by the ease with which God does this. He is so powerful that when He deposes the mighty Babylonian empire it will be with the casual whisk of a broom: "I will sweep her with the broom of destruction" (v. 23). In other words: God's enemies are no big deal.

Message. While my enemies may seem formidable, God can quickly and easily remove them.

Application. Identify any current enemies in my life—sins that entangle me, people out to harm me, situations that batter me. Turn these enemies over to God in prayer, reminding myself that while they are huge to me they are small potatoes to God.

Observation. Note the various words in verses 24–27 that underscore God's sovereignty: *sworn, planned, purposed*. God is not pictured in Isaiah 14 as playing defense. He is not waiting for bad things to happen in our lives and then coming up with a way to rescue us. No, God is large and in charge from the very outset. Everything that would happen to the nations that are described in this section of Isaiah would take place exactly as God had planned it.

Message. God has a plan. Nothing happens outside of that plan or outside of God's control.

Application. When bad things happen to me today—whether they are minor irritations or major catastrophes—say out loud: *God has a plan*. Thank and praise Him for His sovereignty. Sing a song that reminds me that He is on His throne.

Were any of your observations similar to mine in Isaiah 14? There is much more to be gleaned from this chapter than the few things I touched on. And even if you made some of the same observations that I did, you probably drew a different message from one of them and applied it to your life in a way that wouldn't have occurred to me. This is what makes COMA such a rich (and simple) curriculum for small groups to use. When your group gathers each week, even though the members have all been studying the same passages, there will be a wide variety of insights to be shared with one another.

Hebrews 2

Context. The author of this epistle does not identify himself by name. For centuries the church attributed the book to Paul—but that is not likely since Hebrews is written in a style that is very different from Paul's. Whoever penned this letter was well respected in the early church, really knew his Old Testament, and had an intellectually keen mind.

The epistle was addressed to Christians who were in danger of slipping back into Judaism because of persecution. To prevent this from happening, the author drives home the truth that Christ is superior to angels, Moses, Joshua, high priests, and temple sacrifices. Hebrews was most likely written before AD 70 since it does not mention the temple's destruction—an event that would have been of tremendous concern to the author's Jewish-Christian audience.

Observations-Messages-Applications. Here are four observations about Hebrews 2, coupled with corresponding messages and applications.

Observation. Jesus became one of us so that He could come to our rescue. His incarnation is mentioned several times in this chapter (vv. 11, 14, 17–18).

Message. Jesus is not aloof. He desires intimacy with His followers and has gone to great lengths to make it possible.

Application. Take time to praise Christ for becoming a man.

Observation. Jesus was made "perfect" through His suffering (v. 10). Now that's definitely *something striking* since I thought Jesus was perfect to begin with, didn't you? Here's where a footnote can really help. Jesus was never imperfect in a moral or spiritual sense. Being *made perfect* for Jesus involved the completing of His identification with us by going through suffering. This is why Jesus can now serve as our sympathetic high priest (vv. 17–18). He understands the trials we endure and the temptations we face—He's *been there, done that.*

Message. In the words of the old hymn, "Jesus knows our every weakness. . . . Take it to the Lord in prayer" ("What a Friend We Have in Jesus").

Application. What am I troubled about today? What sin is especially tempting me? I need to stop assuming that

Jesus doesn't want to be bothered by these things or wouldn't understand what I'm facing. I should call to mind Jesus' incarnation—and pray!

Observation. God (here's a *truth about* Him) confirmed the preaching of the gospel in New Testament times with signs, wonders, miracles, and gifts of the Holy Spirit (v. 4). Such attestations are still helpful today.

Message. God backs up His *truth* with *proof.*

Application. Cry out to God for my gospel preaching and personal witnessing to be accompanied by displays of His power—especially answers to prayer for the healing of bodies, the restoration of marriages, the provision of jobs, and the deliverance from addictions.

Observation. Jesus came to destroy Satan and deliver people from death—and the fear of death (vv. 14–15).

Message. Jesus can break the stranglehold that Satan has on a person's life.

Application: Who do I know that is currently facing death apart from Christ? I must pray for that individual and make an appointment to meet with them to talk about the One who delivers from death.

There is certainly a lot more to be found in Hebrews 2. By now I hope you're getting the hang of COMA. Don't let go of it when you're finished with *Walk*. Make it your daily practice to be a *doer* of God's Word.

Notes

About the Bible Savvy series
1. Thom S. Rainer, *The Unchurched Next Door* (Grand Rapids: Zondervan, 2003), 200.

Chapter 2: From Text to Life
1. Stephen Covey, *The 7 Habits of Highly Effective People* (New York: Free Press, 2004), 30.
2. A. J. Jacobs, *The Year of Living Biblically: One Man's Humble Quest to Follow the Bible as Literally as Possible* (New York: Simon & Schuster, 2008).

Chapter 4: A Daily Discipline
1. Based on Dave Ramsey, *Financial Peace University* (New York: Penguin Group, 2003).
2. Robert L. Sumner, *The Wonder of the Word of God* (n.p.: Biblical Evangelism Press, 1969).

Bibliography

Ortberg, John. *The Life You've Always Wanted: Spiritual Discipline for Ordinary People*. Grand Rapids: Zondervan, 2002.

Warren, Rick. *Bible Study Methods: Twelve Ways You Can Unlock God's Word*. Grand Rapids: Zondervan, 2006.

Whitney, Donald S. *Spiritual Disciplines for the Christian Life*. Colorado Springs: NavPress, 1991.

JAMES L. NICODEM

Bible Savvy

Epic: The Storyline of the Bible unveils the single theme that ties all of scripture together: redemption.

Foundation: The Trustworthiness of the Bible explains where our current bible came from and why it can be wholly trusted.

Context: How to Understand the Bible shows readers how to read the different parts of the Bible as they were meant to be read and how they fit together.

Walk: How to Apply the Bible puts the readers increased understanding of the Bible into real life terms and contexts.